The Archetypal Plant

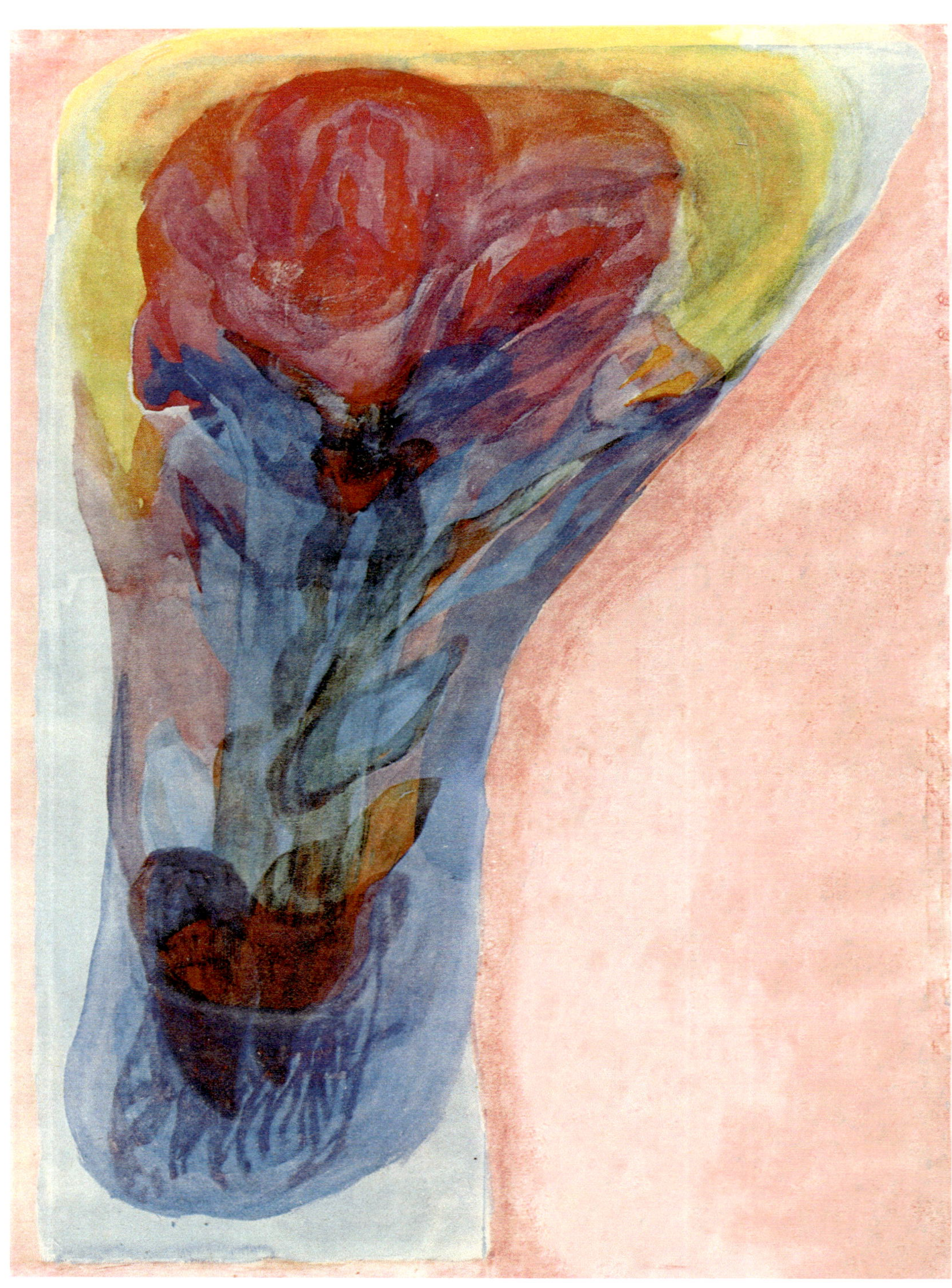

Fig. 1. *The Archetypal Plant* by Rudolf Steiner

The Archetypal Plant

Rudolf Steiner's Watercolour Painting

Angela Lord

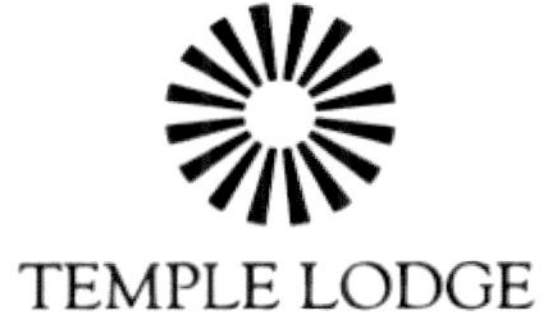

TEMPLE LODGE

Temple Lodge Publishing Ltd.
Hillside House, The Square
Forest Row, RH18 5ES
www.templelodge.com

First published in English by Temple Lodge Publishing, 2015

A CIP catalogue record for this book is available from the British Library

ISBN 978 1 906999 85 8

Typeset and design by Ian Lawton, Hove, East Sussex
Cover by Morgan Creative, featuring detail from 'The Archetypal Plant' by Rudolf Steiner
Printed and bound by 4Edge Ltd.

CONTENTS

LIST OF ILLUSTRATIONS

Unless otherwise stated, all illustrations are by the author.

FOREWORD

"Divinities emerged from flowers:
Brahma, Buddha, Horus
all born from the Lotus,
image of the sun's light upon primeval waters.
Such archetypes uplift us
in the task of modern birth
towards a new awareness
of the divine archetypes living within Nature."
Author

Rudolf Steiner's painting depicts an archetype – the living, dynamic potential which stands behind each individual plant. It lifts us out of the specific genus and provides an image of the growth-forces and formative forces inherent within every plant.

Rudolf Steiner painted the *Archetypal Plant* watercolour in 1924, at a time when research processes by modern scientific methods were being inaugurated.

Nature was under scrutiny, and no longer seen as a whole. Microscopic analysis was subjecting the plant world to an ever-increasing penetrative and specialised examination, with single cells being observed for their chemical responses and reactions. Focussing on the minutiae, such clinical details were becoming more important than the whole plant and its natural environment. Dis-integration, rather than integration, was occurring.

A consequence of this has been the development of objective, non-sympathetic investigations into natural science based on rational detachment. Botanical studies have become increasingly specialised, with plants seeming to belong more to the laboratory than to nature. Genetic technology, for example, with its accompanying agro-chemical industry, seems flawed in its approach, contradictory in application and damagingly polluting.

In spite of all the complexities and skills of modern science, nature and the plant world continue to remain enigmatic. Chemical formulae cannot grow a forest, nor a field of wild flowers. Our contemporary understanding can penetrate the complexities of the infinitesimally small, but somehow nature's secrets continue to elude us, although they do continue to astonish and challenge us.

In the past, Nature was revered and worshipped by humanity, who could see clairvoyantly. Gods and goddesses embodied the living processes of nature, inhabiting the sky, clouds, rain and sun; river and seas; mountains and valleys; forests and fields. No tree was cut down before consulting the protective gods of the forest; no grains were planted or harvested without ritual and ceremony to honour their living source.

Gradually atavistic clairvoyance, which was a natural faculty in earlier stages of human evolution, gave way to an increased perception of the physical world through the senses. The gods, goddesses, nymphs, fauns and satyrs of the ancient world were relegated to the realms of mythology and enchantment. The fairy kingdoms of gnomes, elves, sprites, water, air and fire beings became the creatures of fables and fairytales. Human perception of the world was no longer integrated but became separated into "physical" and "spiritual". The spell of being subjected to the whims of the gods was broken. But another spell was woven, one which has bound humanity into seeing, perceiving and understanding the world of physical matter only.

Researching Rudolf Steiner's *Archetypal Plant* painting can bring about a re-uniting, a reconnecting, of outer sense-perceptions with an inner realm of imaginative cognition, releasing us a little from the spell of matter. To support and enliven such research work, and to help in the building of research processes, we can survey our theme from different aspects:

- from the historical evolutionary relationships we share with plants

- from seeing plants represented in art and architecture

- from the many plant myths and legends which give form and imagination to age-old traditions

- through poetry inspired by flower imagery

- through the cosmic aspects of nature, of earth's relationships to the sun, moon, planets and stars

- by working artistically, to paint the Archetypal Plant motif

- by exploring formative, creative forces of colours and their relationships to plant forms.

In developing this overview we form a deeper more complete picture of the plant world, paying homage to its diverse characteristics, its beauties, its gifts. We thereby acknowledge the enormous significance it has in our lives and the great debt of gratitude and responsibility we owe to it. World-wide concerns regarding ecological imbalance, climatic changes, deforestation and agricultural biodiversity are in the foreground of current international economic and social policies. I am hoping that this book will stimulate new perceptions and develop new perspectives. Through taking a creative approach towards nature we sense its vitality, its fragile abundance and acknowledge that its essence is our essence, and that its health and well-being is inseparable from our own health and well-being.

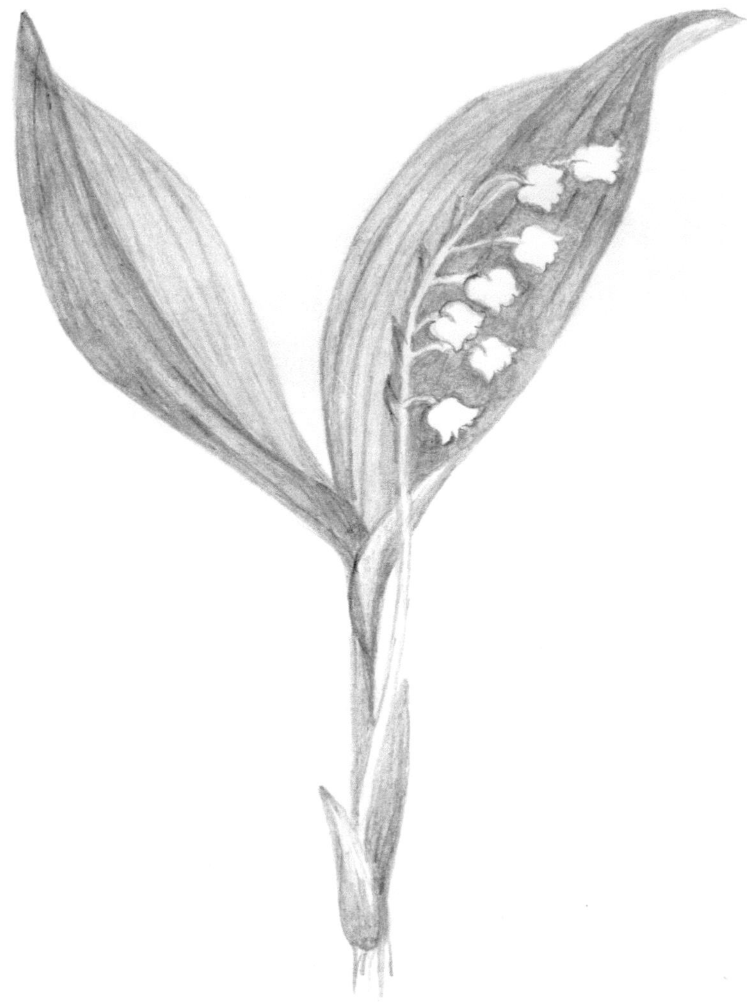

Fig 2. *Lily of the Valley*, drawing by author

PART ONE

CHAPTER ONE: THE DISTANT PAST

"And God said, Let the Earth put forth vegetation, plants yielding seed, and fruit trees bearing fruit in which is their seed, each according to its own kind, upon the earth. And it was so".

Genesis 1:2

In his book *Cosmic Memory, Atlantis and Lemuria*, Rudolf Steiner describes a time of early earthly evolution in the following way: "In earlier stages of earth evolution when the human being was not yet physical, he/she existed as astral and etheric substances. The actions of stones, plants and animals (which then also only existed as astral forms), were felt as inner soul experiences. At this time, the sun, the earth and the moon were not separated from each other. During an early evolutionary phase (known as 'the Sun phase'), the 'physical' human body, which was only as dense as a gaseous substance, had a plant-like cloud existence. Certain organs of the human body retained plant-like characteristics until the beginning of the Earth evolutionary phase." [1]

From this description we can understand that stones, plants, animals and humans were at one time all intimately united in a non-physical state of existence. The cloud-like substance and form of the human being was made up of delicate floating structures which were able to "sense" the interpenetrating animals, plants and mineral substances, which also consisted of non-physical material.

Aeons later, after the sun had separated from the earth, but when the earth and moon were still united, the form of the plant consisted mainly of roots. The downward thrust of the plant's root system spread out powerfully, while above the earth's surface, the plant only peeped out. The "earth" was volatile, with extensive volcanic activity, very high temperatures and steamy, swampy conditions.

Human cloud-forms, with their loose floating plant-like characteristics were illustrated by Rudolf Steiner. Here we can see what may be termed as the "Cosmic human being", which existed in a nebulous form until the evolutionary phase known as early Lemuria. (See illustration overleaf.)

1. Rudolf Steiner, *Cosmic Memory, Atlantis and Lemuria,* Chapter 8.

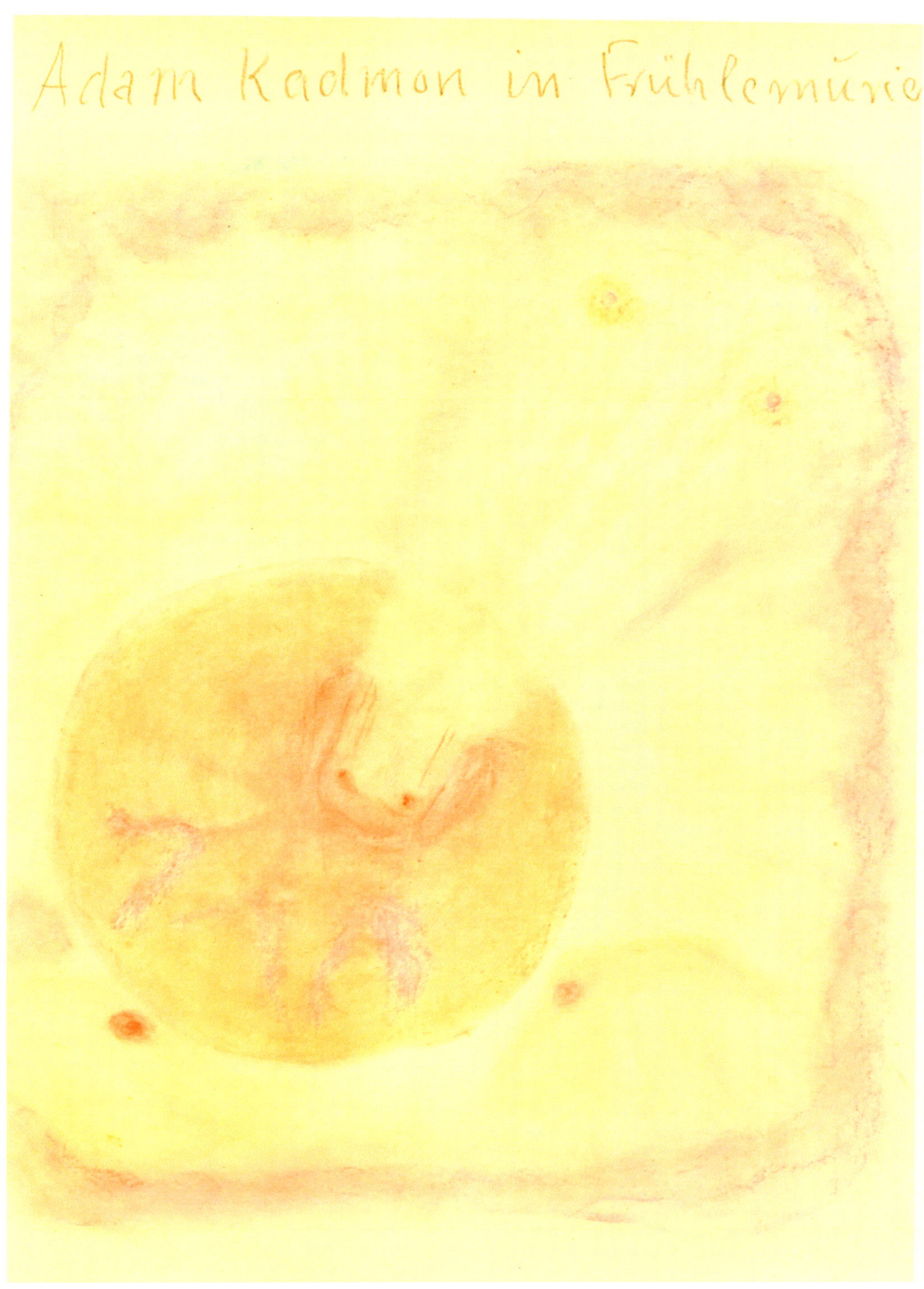

Fig. 3. *Adam Kadmon in Early Lemuria* by Rudolf Steiner

When the moon separated from the earth, after a time of great upheaval, there unfolded, in what was previously only tiny shoots peeping out into the world, a longing for the wide light-filled spaces of the cosmos. This "longing" in the plant brought about the flowers and the process of blossoming. In a way, the departure of the moon was a kind of liberation for the plants, enabling them to develop forces of growth and to rise up out of the enveloping earthly substances.

Gradually stones, plants and animals became differentiated, and the once unified human being now separated into male and female, Adam and Eve. Their expulsion from Paradise denotes a "fall" into the sense world – they could see their nakedness. Meanwhile different stages of earth's evolution gave rise to various types of plant growth. To quote again from Cosmic Memory, we read that during this time of Lemuria: "The world of plants ... resembled our palms and similar trees ... At that time our ferns were trees and formed mighty forests ... What exists now in small forms was then developed in gigantic sizes. In their temples the (later) Lemurian people participated in direct contemplation of the active forces of Nature.

They experienced a communion with the beings, the gods, which built the world itself. Women developed special powers related to their faculty of imagination, which was in alliance with Nature. This became the basis for a higher development of the life of ideas, forming the beginnings of memory, and the capacity to form the first and simplest moral concepts. Men were active in the realm of the Will, having power over the strength within their own bodies they had the ability to endure pain and hardship. They were, in a way, magicians of the Will, seeing and exercising the forces of Nature."[2]

The continent of Lemuria was sited on our present Indian Ocean, extending from North Africa to Southern Australia, and covering an area which included Ceylon, Madagascar, Borneo, Sumatra and Java, stretching into the South-West Pacific. Flora and fauna on these islands in our present day, display on a small scale, similarities to the gigantic plant forms which flourished in Lemurian times, but little physical evidence of this continent remains. However, oil reserves beneath the earth's surface in various parts of the world are constituted from these mighty forests. Fossils of large plant forms and the many types of prehistoric animals originate from the later stages of the Lemurian phase.[3]

During the period of evolution which followed, when the fabled civilisation of Atlantis existed in what is now the Atlantic Ocean area, a remarkable relationship between the Atlantean people and the plant kingdom developed. Rudolf Steiner, in *Cosmic Memory*, writes:

"The Atlantean could change the energy of a pile of grain into technical power...

2. Ibid. Chapter 5.
3. Known as the Mesozoic or Mesolithic time (10,000 – 8,000 BC).

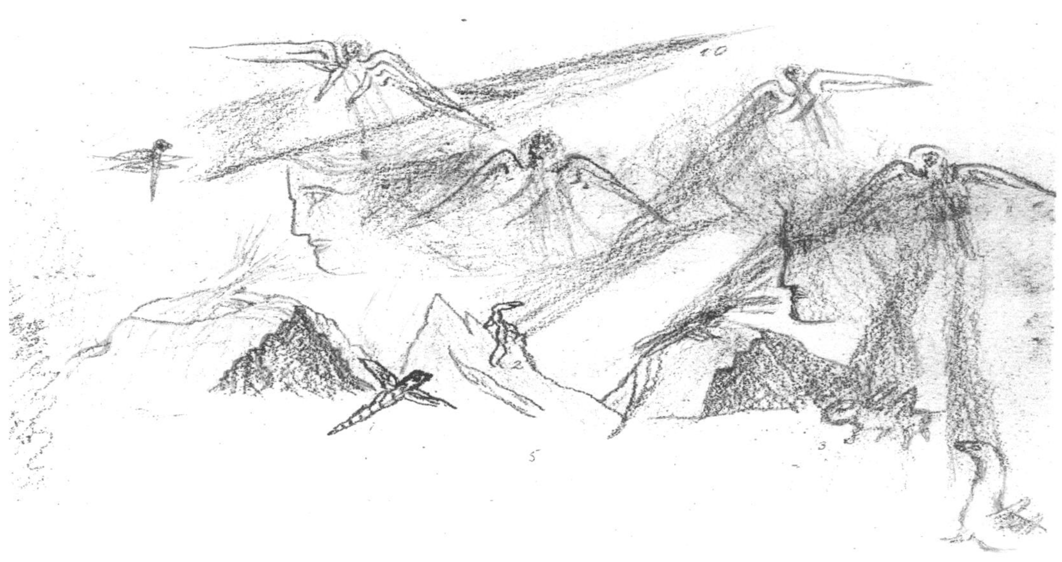

Fig. 4. Lemuria, pencil sketch for the first Goetheanum ceiling, Rudolf Steiner

Plants were cultivated in the Atlantean period not only for use as foodstuffs but also in order to make the energies dormant in them available to commerce and industry ...” [4]

Later Atlantean sub-races, however, began to use these powers to satisfy their own wishes and desires. This manipulation of nature's forces to produce energy for the wrong purposes led ultimately to a series of catastrophic climatic changes which we know of as the Ice Ages, finally ending in the Great Flood as recorded in the Bible.

Since Plato's time there has been speculation over this mysterious continent of Atlantis, and many attempts have been made to prove its existence. In the next chapter we will look at a fascinating and puzzling phenomena, the Green Man, which may possibly be connected to this legendary civilisation, or at least, to the atavistic consciousness which was the normal human condition at that time.

4. Op. cit., Chapter 3, 'Our Atlantean Ancestors'.

CHAPTER TWO: THE "GREEN MAN" IMAGE

> "And he saw a youth approaching
> Dressed in garments green and yellow
> Through the splendour of the sunset
> Plumes of green bent o'er his forehead
> And his hair was soft and golden ...
>
> ... All around the happy village
> Stood the maize-fields, green and shining,
> Waved the green plumes of Mondamin,
> Waved his soft and sunny tresses
> Filling all the land with plenty ..."
>
> from *Hiawatha*, H. W. Longfellow

Sculptured reliefs, often found as features in older churches, depict human male heads with leaves instead of hair and with leaves bursting out of their nostrils, mouths, and sometimes even their eyes. They are known as the "Green Men" and have been a source of fascination and speculation for hundreds of years, providing us with an enchanting and challenging mystery. Depictions of the Green Man appear as decorative architectural features as far afield as Borneo, India, Nepal, Iraq, Lebanon, throughout central Europe and throughout the British Isles, making his presence known in Jain, Buddhist, Middle Eastern, Roman and Christian traditions.

Although pagan or pre-Christian in origin, the motif can be found in the church from as early as the fourth and fifth centuries AD. Even as late as the twelfth and thirteenth centuries the image continued to be developed through variations of the antique, becoming an unusual but integral part of the church's symbolic language. Originally the Green Man was portrayed surrounded by, and speaking or breathing the acanthus leaf. Gradually other foliage was depicted, particularly from plants such as the hawthorn, growing in northern Europe, and in Britain distinctive oak leaves were also featured. Early churches have Green Men carved into capitals; by the Middle Ages they were included as decorative details on vaulted ceilings, or corbels and cornices, carved in both stone and wood, sometimes brightly painted. They can also be found as decorative features on the ends of pews in choir stalls and congregational seating.

But who are Green Men and where do they come from? By delving back into the distant past, we can trace a few leading insights as to their possible origins.

In his book *Cosmic Memory, Atlantis and Lemuria*, Rudolf Steiner describes a powerful and intimate connection which humanity once shared with the plant kingdom during the time of Atlantis. The Atlantean people had more malleable physical bodies than we have in our present-day, as did animals and plants. Rudolf Steiner describes how during the early stages of Atlantis, the development of language took place, and that with this development a bond was established between the human soul and everything external to it. The soul powers of these first Atlanteans still possessed something of the forces of nature, and the spoken words which they produced had a similar potency to nature. They not only named things, but in their words was a power over things, and also over their fellow-men. When a word was pronounced it developed a power similar to that of the object it designated, hence words had an effect – they could influence the growth of plants or tame wild animals. These early Atlanteans (known as the Rmoahals) felt that this was a revered gift of nature, and therefore language was sacred. The misuse of certain sounds was not possible, as they felt that misuse would cause great harm, and in a state of naïve innocence they ascribed their power not so much to themselves as to divine nature acting within them. A settlement at this time was completely in alliance with nature, resembling a garden in which houses were built with artfully intertwined branches. Everything which the work of human hands created, grew out of nature. Atlanteans could control what is termed "the life force", transforming the germinal energy of plant seeds into the service of their technology, so plants were cultivated for use as foodstuffs as well as to utilise energies dormant within seeds for commerce and industry.

Initiate leaders communicated with higher spiritual beings so that they could guide humanity with the wisdom which they received in the temples of the mysteries. The supernatural-divine revealed itself through Initiation-wisdom, so that the thoughts and labours of humanity would serve the invisible spiritual worlds, based on divine administration. New cultures and civilisations came into being under the legendary great priest kings of pre-history. Some evidence of this is to be found in the Old Testament of the Bible, in Genesis, Chapter 6, where a reference is made to a co-mingling of races at the time of Noah. We read: "The Nephilim were on the earth in those days and also afterward, when the sons of God came into the daughters of men, and they bore children to them. These were the mighty men that were of old, the men of renown."

Gradually this reverential state of consciousness changed. Ambition and personal value began to grow with a heightened sense of personality. Selfishness led to the power over nature being put at the service of personal egotism. This destructive effect was only curtailed through the development of higher faculties, namely logical thinking and judgement, which stabilised the run-away wishes and desires but only to a certain extent.

The result was the development of a powerfully magical and manipulative technology. This misuse of knowledge and selfish manipulation of nature led eventually to mighty forces being unleashed. Unpredictable reactions in the use of germinal forces in plant seeds resulted in catastrophic events. Natural elemental powers of the weather raged violently out of control causing immense and widespread devastation. Flooding and massive storms led to the sinking of the whole continent with the consequent destruction of virtually all life. These disastrous catastrophes are known as the Ice Ages, and are referred to in the Bible (and other cultural traditions) as the Great Flood.

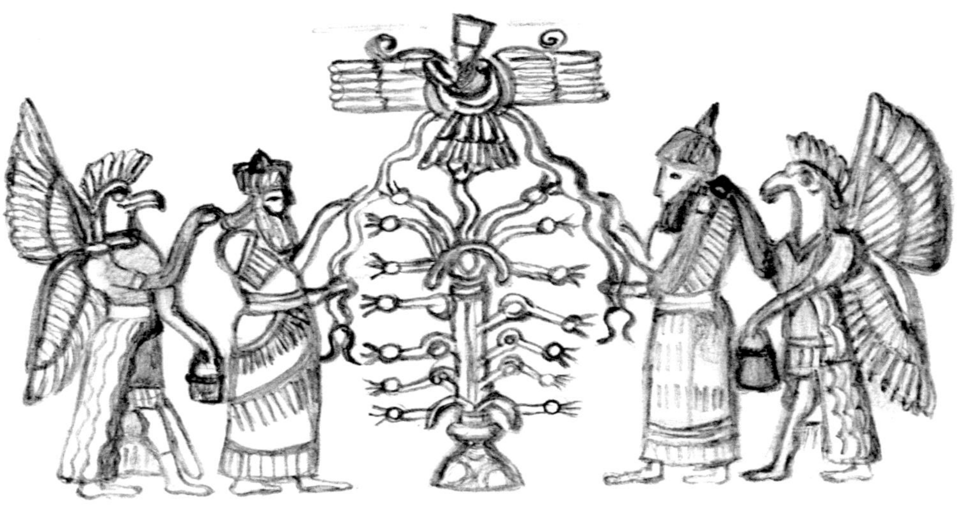

Fig. 5.   Imprint from Neo-Assyrian cylinder seal showing a king, a priest, and bird-headed winged figures beside a sacred tree. Pencil drawing by author. It could be questioned as to whether this is actually a tree or perhaps a technological energy device.

Now, to return to our Green Man, bearing in mind the attributes of humanity in Atlantean times. It seems somehow possible that the Green Man could be an image representing our Atlantean ancestors, speaking and breathing the language of the plants. Interestingly some Green Men have rather unnerving expressions on their faces and in their eyes. They seem to convey something tragic, with on occasions, anguished looks in their eyes. They appear to be trapped within the foliage suffering immense inner despair. We can ask – what are they seeing? What are they experiencing? Perhaps these haunting expressions of fear, even terror, bear a silent witness to once-seen and once-experienced tragedies. These Green Men speak freely through their mouths but their eyes are fearful.

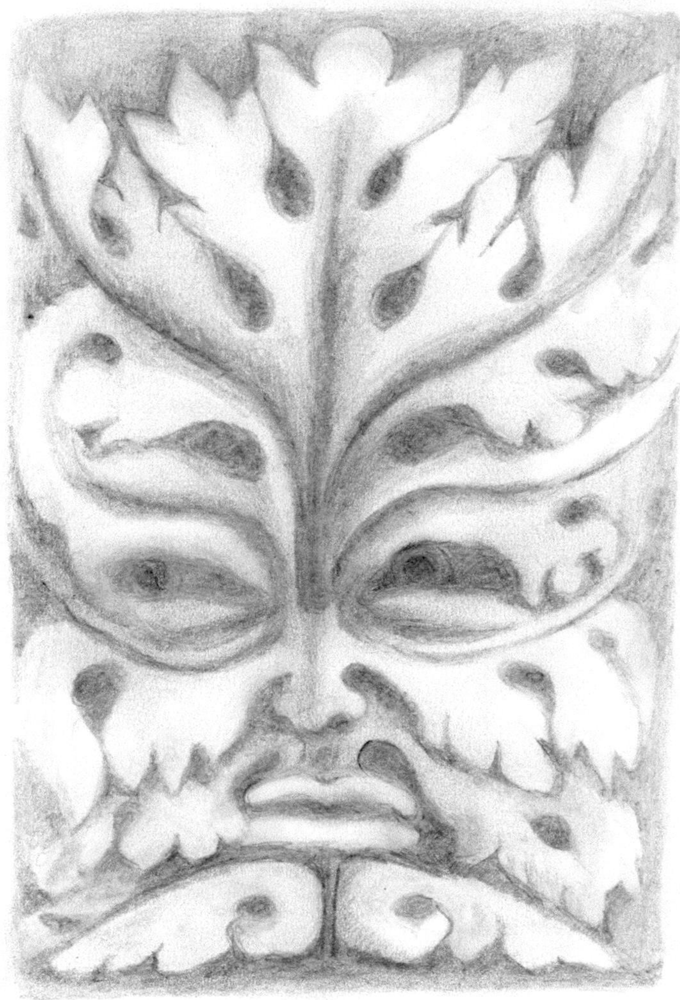

Fig. 6.   Bamberg Cathedral, the acanthus-leaf Green Man. Detail below the Rider Statue, circa
           1237. Drawing author's own.

Our enigma includes questions as to why they are placed within the context of
religious tradition, and why the church has deemed it necessary that such strange
images feature repeatedly amongst the usual Christian imagery.   Did the early
church wish to acknowledge the atavistic powers and potent magic of the past?
Was this an attempt at synthesizing pagan practices with Christianity? Perhaps they
serve as a reminder that disobeying the laws of nature can bring about disaster, with
Green Men symbolically representing the use and eventual misuse of the spoken
word in ancient times. The church would encourage obedience to God's laws as

set down in the scriptures so that the wisdom of the word of God and obedience to it would hopefully become a safeguard for humanity in the future.   Human greed and manipulatively ambitious misuse of plant forces destroyed an ancient and sophisticated civilisation. Elemental beings and the natural energy potential stored within seeds were so misused that war was waged on humanity ("God's punishment for their Sins"). God's promise to Noah and other initiates who guided survivors to various parts of the world , and to all subsequent civilisations, is that this would not happen again.

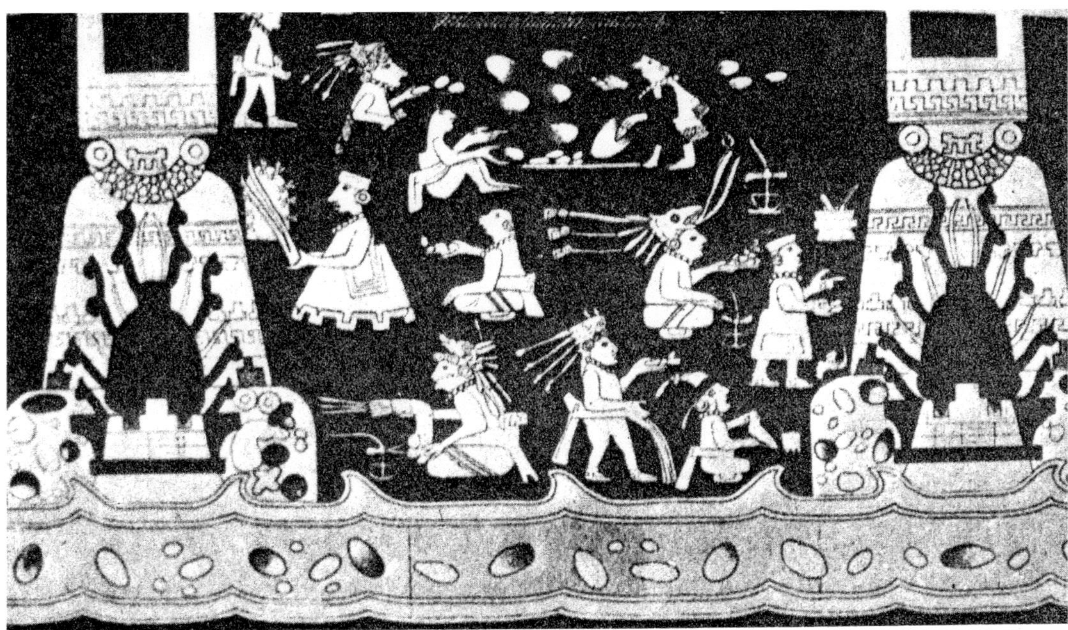

Fig. 7. Teotihuacanos bring seeds to unusually shaped structures. Could these be types of furnaces? Wall painting from the Hall of Agriculture, near the Pyramids of the Sun and Moon, Teotihuacan, Mexico. From: Flavio Conti, *Centres of Belief (The grand tour)*, publ. Cassell, London 1977.

In the Bible two particular signs signified the end of the Flood, namely, the dove carrying the olive branch, and the rainbow miraculously set in the sky after the deluge had cleared as a covenant between God and mankind. In Genesis, Chapter 8, we read: " ... again he sent forth the dove out of the ark; and the dove came back to him in the evening, and lo, in her mouth, a freshly picked olive leaf. So Noah knew that the waters had subsided from the earth."

These two signs have provided us with profoundly meaningful emblems: the rainbow signifying hope in a colourfully luminous bridge spanning heaven and earth; and the white dove carrying an olive branch which has become a universal symbol for peace.

It's probably not possible to answer the questions posed in this chapter, however much we would like everything to be clarified. This area of research is one which, for the time being, remains open, eluding any firm conclusion. We can consider however, that the power of language contains far-reaching effects, and perhaps the Green Man reminds us that words can both create and destroy. We read, in the Gospel of St John, Chapter 1:

> And the Word was with God
> And the Word was God
> He was in the beginning with God
> And all things were made through him.

Words heal and harm; sound can magically break matter down (or technologically do so). Sounds can also alter consciousness, for example in the practice of chanting mantric tones and verses, or in the singing of medieval plainsong and hymns.

A final consideration is the implication that disrespect for nature (especially "in the name of science") has consequences which are not quite forseeable or predictable. Our present climate changes are perhaps signalling that there is a need to reconsider our approach to the world and its resources. This may not be the first time we have been in such a situation.

CHAPTER THREE: FROM ATLANTIS TO DEMETER

> "... Now as for comparing mankind to grains of corn.
> In every man who is healthy and natural there is a
> germinating force as in a grain of wheat. And so
> natural life is germination. Now what the germinating
> force is in the grain of wheat, love is in us....."
>
> Vincent van Gogh, Paris, 1887
> Excerpt from a letter to his sister Wilhelmina.

Civilisations which developed after the Great Flood bore Mystery-traditions which had originated in Atlantean times. Nature was experienced intimately, and these experiences were incorporated within the many gods and goddesses revered in the Egyptian and the Greek Mysteries.

One such deity is the Greek goddess, Demeter, whose origins can be traced back to the time of Atlantis. The Atlanteans' clairvoyant experiences of nature were not limited to only super-sensory perceptions, but extended to an awareness that in the processes of eating and digesting, the plant kingdom was actually building up their physical body and their consciousness.

Rudolf Steiner said that "... when an Atlantean man gazed into the Spiritual worlds, he saw Demeter; she really came to meet him ..."

"... Demeter is the ruler of the greatest Wonders of Nature. She is an archetypal form which points to a time when the life of the human brain was not yet cut off from the general bodily life, a time when nutrition by external foodstuffs and thinking through the instrument of the brain were not separate functions. When the crops were thriving in the fields it was still felt at that time that thinking was alive there, that hope was outpoured over the fields and penetrated the activity of Nature's wonder like the song of the lark. It was still felt that along with material substance, spiritual life is absorbed into the human body, becomes purified, becomes spirit – as the archetypal mother, out of whom what is born elementally becomes Persephone in the human being himself ..."

"The great nature-goddess Demeter sent forces into the human soul, where they were worked upon and became transformed into the faculty of clairvoyance. The Atlantean felt this clairvoyant capacity born in him as the birth of Persephone".[1]

From these insights, we can understand that in Greek mythology, the abduction of Persephone by Pluto is the process by which the faculty of clairvoyance gradually, in the course of evolution, becomes subconscious. Persephone is held in the underworld through the gradual densification of the human body. As the human

1. Rudolf Steiner, *Wonders of the World*, Lecture 1.

body became more and more estranged from Nature, the spiritual moral laws which were previously imparted directly through bodily nutrition needed to be bestowed in a new way. A more intellectual morality was given through the Mysteries, especially at Eleusis. Here the gods could convey their spiritual wisdom through the initiate priests and priestesses who established rites and ceremonies forming the basis of the cultural-spiritual life in the great civilisations which developed throughout the ancient world.

The abduction of Persephone is also interpreted as an explanation for the changes in the four seasons of the year, and the rhythmical cycle of spring, summer, autumn and winter. this is perhaps the outer, or exoteric, association with nature, whereas the esoteric intention was to represent the winter of the human soul.

The Story of Demeter and Persephone

Demeter was the goddess who more than any other embodied for the Greeks the reality of the fruitful earth. She was an ancient deity, the corn-goddess on whom survival depended. In later times she was also the sorrowing mother of Persephone. When out picking flowers in a meadow with her companions, Persephone had been seen by Hades. Suddenly inflamed with love (having been struck by an arrow from Eros), Hades swept her away in his chariot. He caused a great chasm to open before them in the earth and carried her down to his underworld kingdom. Persephone's companions looked on helplessly. Demeter searched everywhere for her daughter, neglecting the earth so that it ceased to be fruitful. Zeus, the great ruler and father of the Gods, had to intervene lest the earth become completely barren, and mankind perish. His messenger, Hermes, conducted Persephone back to her mother at Eleusis, where she could have stayed had she not eaten the food of the dead – four pomegranate seeds – which bound her to Hades forever. Through Zeus' intervention, Hades exacted a compromise: for each of the seeds she had eaten, she would spend a month with him, the remainder of the year she could spend with Demeter her mother. Thus did fertility return to the earth, spring blossomed and grains flourished, but when Persephone returned to Hades, winter fell upon the land.

For readers who may be more familiar with the Romanised names, they are as follows:

Demeter	Ceres (= our word cereal)
Persephone	Prosperpina
Zeus	Jupiter
Hades	Pluto
Eros	Cupid
Hermes	Mercury

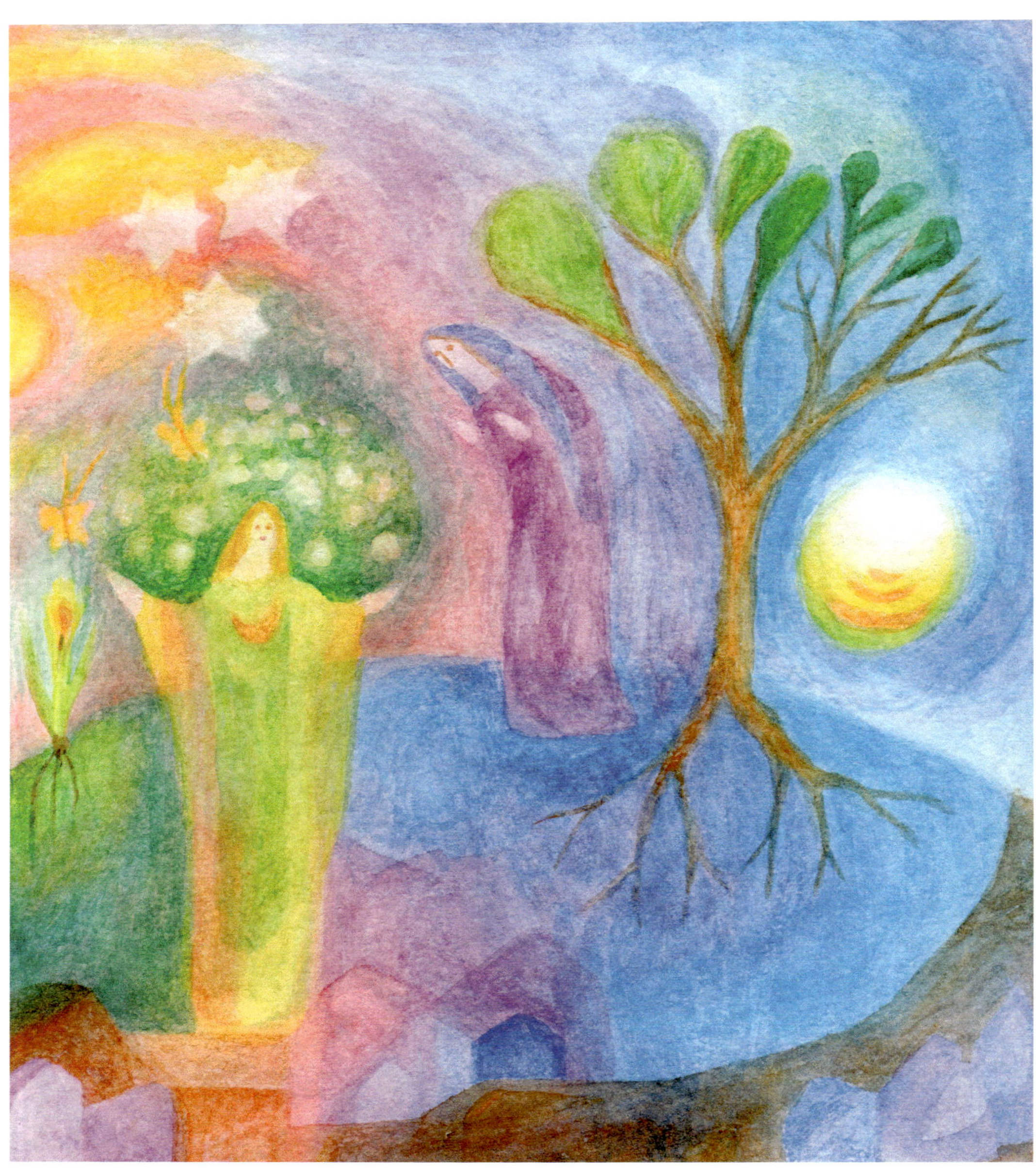

Fig. 8. *Demeter and Persephone* (author)

CHAPTER FOUR:
SACRED ARCHITECTURE AND PICTORIAL SYMBOL

"Thou art the Iris, fair among the fairest,
who, armed with golden rod
And winged with the celestial azure, bearest
the message of some God ...

...O flower-de-luce, bloom on, and let the river
linger to kiss thy feet!
O flower of song, bloom on, and make forever
the world more fair and sweet."

from *Beautiful Lily*, Longfellow

Since pre-history trees have been worshipped as the actual dwelling place of the gods, as the home of nature deities, and as physical embodiments of guardian spirits whose benevolent presence within the tree bestowed protection over the surrounding forests and fields. Egyptian mother-goddesses, for example, were incorporated into trees, and long before they built stone temples the Greeks worshipped their gods in sacred groves of trees, or in sacred fields. Many of the gods and goddesses were ascribed their own special tree, for example, Zeus was embodied within the oak; Apollo, the great sun god, was worshipped within the laurel, the olive and the palm; Aphrodite was connected to the myrtle, Athena to the olive tree, and Dionysos to the vine.

Every ancient culture has its individual, and yet at the same time a universal tradition of revering spirit-imbued trees. The New Zealand Maoris named their giant Kauri trees "Lord of the Forest" and, before any could be cut down for canoe or house-building, ritual prayers were spoken. Firstly to ask permission and secondly to free the spirit within the tree.

"Those who followed the old lore respected the spirit of everything. They did not cut down a tree without asking *Taane Mahuta*[1] for its life. And permission was not always given. Nothing was taken from the forest or the waters without the agreement of the guardians. Furthermore, in taking there was restoration. When a tall tree was felled for a *waka*[2] it was replaced by fifteen seedlings and the *Tohunga* (the wisdom keeper) presiding over the felling was responsible for their nurture until they could stand alone in the wind. Nothing was taken to the detriment of the spirit."[3]

1. God of trees and birds.
2. Canoe.
3. Barry Brailsford, *Song of the Stone*, Chapter 2, 'The Trail of the Deer – Listen to the Land'.

Concerning the Greek consciousness of the past, Rudolf Steiner wrote, "The contrast between nature and spirit which we today experience was unknown to the Greeks. When they looked at the processes which took place in wood and meadow, in sun and moon, in the world of the stars, they did not yet experience a natural existence devoid of spirit, but everything which happened in the world was the deed of spiritual beings ... In those ancient times Spirit and Nature were in full harmony with one another." [4]

Natural atavistic clairvoyance enabled priests to carry out rituals in the actual places where they were able to see and sense the presence of nature spirits. Ritual sacrifices were an integral part of ancient religious practice, involving dance, music and processions. Animals and humans were honoured in the act of giving their life forces as a sacrifice to the gods or to consecrate a sacred site. Trees and groves were then decorated with the implements used in such rituals, together with the sacrificial remains which created a potentised spiritual "substance", enhancing an area in an atmosphere both sacred and strange, and imbuing the site with potent life-forces.

Early temples to Artemis were constructed of trees. Philostratus refers to her forest shrines made in the old style, of tree trunks, which were decorated with sacred weapons of the hunt in her honour.

At a later stage of nature-worship, trees were often trimmed into the shape of primitive columns. Archaeological evidence shows that early temples were actually made of solid wooden columns. Each wooden temple column would be sacred, and may have been worshipped for the etheric life-forces within it. According to Pausanias, the first temple to Apollo at Delphi was a hut of laurel trees. Remnants of these nature perceptions, which grew from an ancient form of atavistic consciousness, have been handed down through time in the myths and legends to be found in almost every folklore in the world.

In Ovid (*Metamorphoses*, 10 – 725), Venus consecrates the anemone that Adonis has become, and calls it a monument. Carya, the daughter of King Dion of Laconia, was punished by Dionysos for spurning his love. He turned her into a walnut tree.

Such evocative legends were experienced as "nature-realities", but with the fading clairvoyance and the development of independent thoughts and perceptions, the Greeks found it necessary to step away from their direct unimpeded relationship to nature, and to begin to construct the marvellous stone temples for which they are famed. Their gods and goddesses became embodied in stone, marble and metal in magnificent works of sculptural art.

4. Rudolf Steiner, *Wonders of the World,* Lecture 3.

Rites and rituals were enacted within the sacred precincts of carved marble sanctuaries and halls. Greek art and architecture as we know it had its beginnings in the fact that fading clairvoyance gave rise to a sense of separation from nature, and a longing to revere her, even perhaps to hold fast to her. Nature remained stable and present within stone. Temple architecture would provide new and wondrous homes for the gods and goddesses to dwell in, places so beautiful that by their very proportion the gods would find them irresistible, and would fill them with divine presence.

During early Christian times, a mixture of naïve and sophisticated imagery existed. The power of observation of nature which was awakening in about 500 BCE, was put to sleep again by 500 AD. Artists no longer checked their formulae and images against reality. However, portraits although stylised were instantly recognisable, as were animals and birds, but plants were more decorative, rather than botanical. Something of an archetypal gesture was used to indicate a tree, a bush or a flower. Occasionally one could name a particular species, but the plant kingdom, on the whole, was utilised in order to portray a pleasing earthly setting. In this way, artists were expressing what they felt, as conveying an inner soul-mood was considered to be more important now, than outer accuracy.

Plant forms were also used in Christian symbolism in early Christian art, as they could be readily adapted from existing pagan symbols. Vines, for example, which had previously suggested life now represented Christ as the true vine; fruits and flowers which as pre-Christian images provided nourishment in the after-life of the deceased, now became symbols of the abundance of eternal life in Christ. Vines,

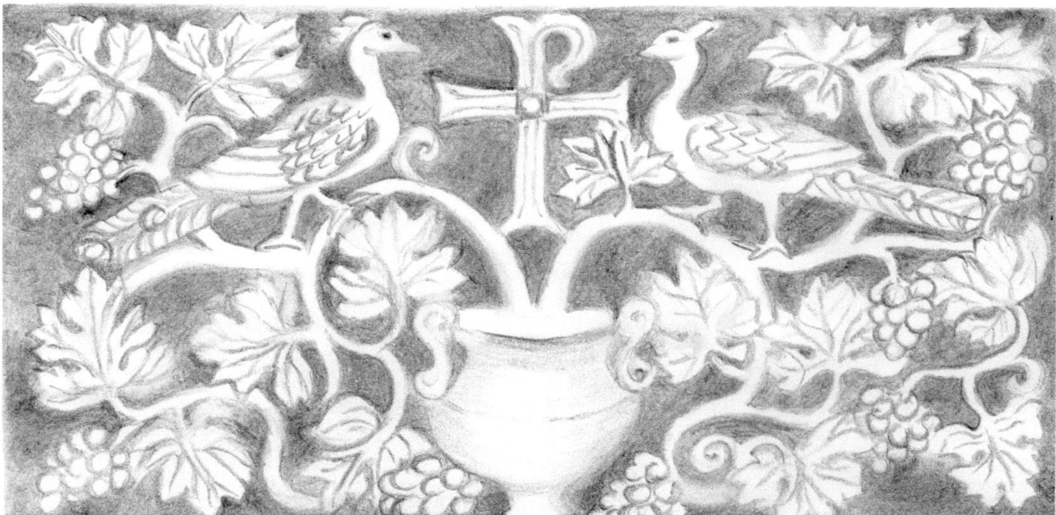

Fig. 9. Decorative relief, Sant Apollinare Nuovo, Ravenna. Drawing by author. Source: *Christian Symbols*

leaves and bunches of grapes decorate baptismal fonts and eucharist chalices, representing the renewal of life.

The Tree of Jesse symbol is found in the prophecy of Isaiah, in Chapter 11: "And there shall come forth a rod out of the root of Jesse, and a flower shall rise up out of his root. And the Spirit of the Lord shall rest upon him, the spirit of wisdom and of understanding, the spirit of counsel and of fortitude, the spirit of knowledge and of godliness." The rod (or rood) was a symbol for the Virgin Mary, and the flower represented Jesus, later, the Christ.

The sacredness and beauty of the plant kingdom was acknowledged through all of Christendom. Something physical and natural was at the same time, super-physical and super-natural. An immediate dependency upon Nature was a reality in the Middle Ages, and her divinity was acknowledged throughout the skilled hands and imaginatively inspired artists and craftsmen of this time.

From the seventh to the twelfth centuries, painters and illustrators of illuminated manuscripts developed animals and plant-inspired forms to embellish borders and lettering. Complex, rhythmical, and meticulously detailed, winding interlaced vines, leaves and delicate flowers conveyed an ordering of nature's randomness. The harmonious geometrical basis of plant structures were so emphasized that nature's rhythms were readily held or set into intricately ordered designs.

Rather than depicting abstract geometrical patterns, the European artists of illuminated manuscripts utilised the inherent geometry which is visible within plant growth and form. We see this echoed in wood and stone, in the sculptural element of church and monastical architectural features, as well as in the many decorative ornamentations of furnishings; religious objects (such as reliquaries, baptismal fonts and candlesticks); coloured stained-glass windows, and embroidered robes.

The intricate interweaving of designs based on plant forms in illuminated manuscripts (especially in the capital letters which open a new Biblical chapter or begin a new prayer), are particularly interesting. Their elaborate criss-crossing, when carefully traced, leads in an unbroken pattern from beginning to end. A rhythmic movement weaving from left to right, up and down, through diagonal interlacings, can be traced in a continuous thread. This seems to hint at the unbroken weaving threads of life which weave within and behind the events of nature and of life itself.

The following quotation conveys a poetical humanistic medieval perception of nature's divinity and order.

"Divine Providence ... reviewed the resources of her mind, mustered her faculties, and summoned up her imaginative powers ... She imposed law and restrained their freedom of motion ... she effected a balance of properties among her undisciplined and recalcitrant materials, joined them with means, and so bound them together in arithmetical proportion. as the bonds of a reconciling concord, sprung from the inner deliberations of Providence, were thus interposed, the rough and uncivilised strain in matter changed its obstinacy to cooperation ... Once this rigidity of ancient, even primordial lineage had been overcome, an adaptability took its place capable of being drawn into such channels as Providence decreed ...

"When these necessary steps had been taken with regard to matter, when the framework of the elements was now solidly established, the outward shape of creation made beautiful and its coherence become a very miracle, Noys turned her intelligence to the production of a cosmic soul. She was the fountain of light, seed-bed of life, a good born of the divine goodness, that fullness of knowledge which is called the 'mind' of the most high ...

"There, in a clearer glass, might be seen all that God's hidden will would bring to pass through temporal generation or by divine act. There were enrolled, in kind, in species, in individual uniqueness, all that the cosmic order, that the elements labour to bring forth. There, inscribed by the finger of the supreme arbiter, were the fabric of time, the chain of destiny, the disposition of the ages."[5]

5. 'Megacosmus', from the *Cosmographia of Bernardus Silvestris*, Chapter 2 (written 1140-45).

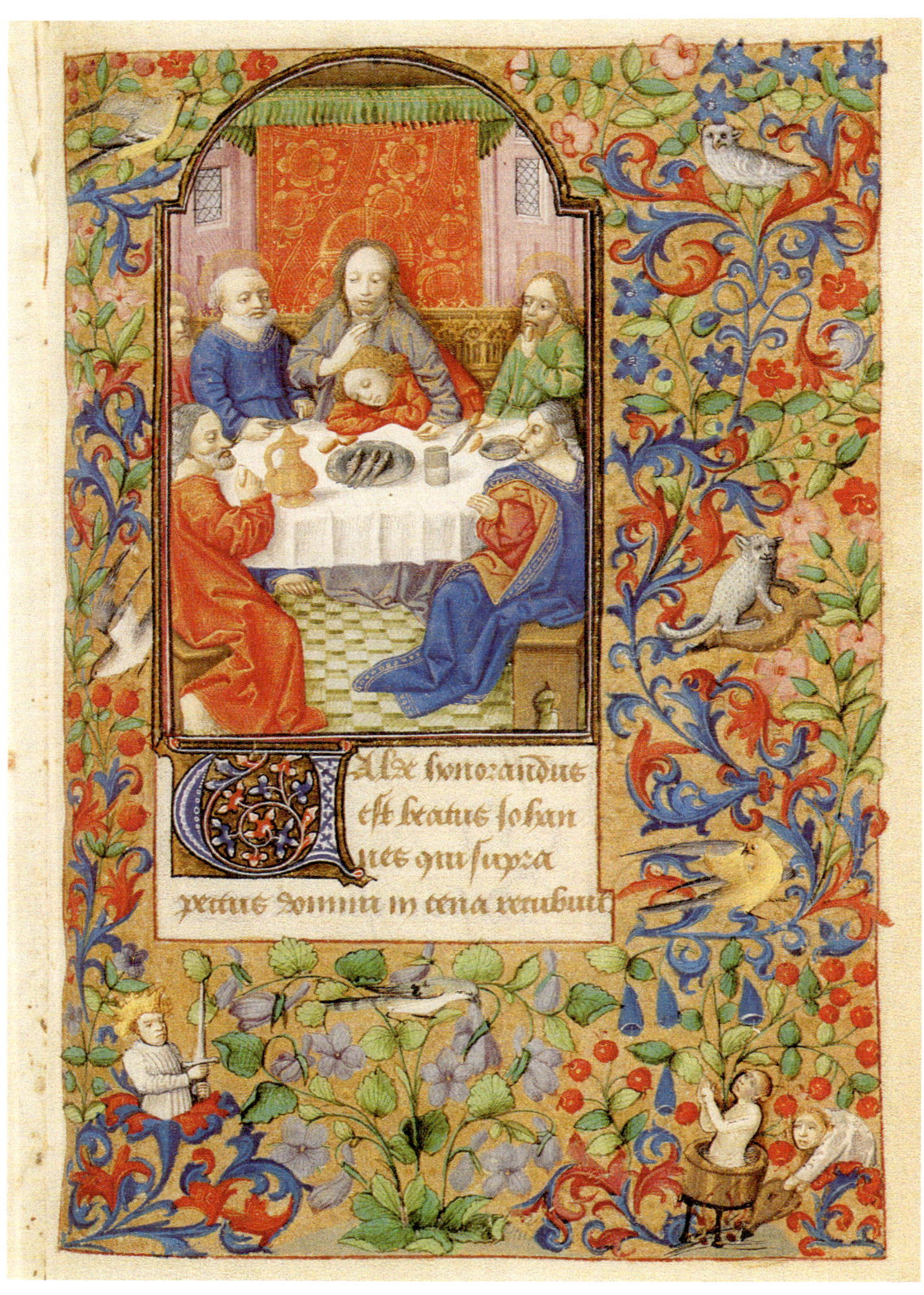

Fig. 10. The Last Supper, from the *Margaret de Foix Book of Hours*, France, c. 1470. V & A

PART TWO

CHAPTER ONE: THE FLOWER AS SYMBOL

The beauty of flowers, their colours, forms and fragrances enrich our lives – they delight our senses and our souls, bringing life and freshness, they provide an accompaniment to all of our passages or rituals in life and in death. Births, christenings (or baptisms), birthdays, engagements, weddings, anniversaries and funerals are celebrated and acknowledged with floral tributes.

Cultural, religious and seasonal festivals throughout the world are embellished with flowers; they speak a silent universal language that every open-minded and open-hearted person can hear. Flowers are associated with feelings of joy, tenderness, gratitude, love and comfort. Conveying their beautiful eloquence appropriately for all situations they speak on our behalf: to celebrate, to congratulate, to apologise, to console. It is really not without reason that we have the expression "to say it with flowers". Our innermost soul seems to find its mirror and its expression within their beautiful forms, fragrances and colours.

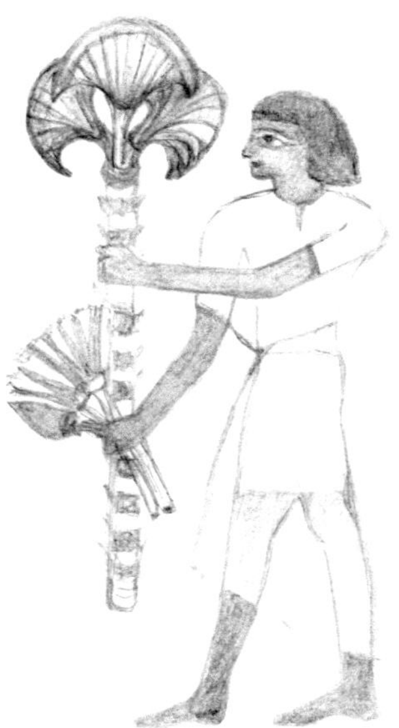

Fig. 11. Flower Offering. From an Egyptian tomb painting, Thebes, eighteenth Dynasty (author's drawing)

Flowers are also symbols for states of consciousness. Buds, for example, denote potential, something which is about to unfold (e.g. a budding genius, or a budding beauty). They symbolise youthfulness, purity, naïvety and innocence – all that which is still closed off and protected from worldly influences. Buds evoke tenderness; for example, Shakespeare wrote of "the darling buds of May".

The opened flower is a symbol of development, of unfolding, of opening. It references cultural progress, the soul-life and spiritual awareness, all of which are portrayed either symbolically or metaphorically by the opened flower (e.g. the bloom of youth; a blossoming romance; the flowering of the Renaissance). The opened lotus flower signified spiritual enlightenment and the opening of the chakras, each chakra having a certain number of spiritual lotus petals. The six-petalled lotus can also represent the macrocosm, while the five-petalled flowers (the rose, for example), can be images used to convey the microcosm of man contained within the boundaries of the senses.

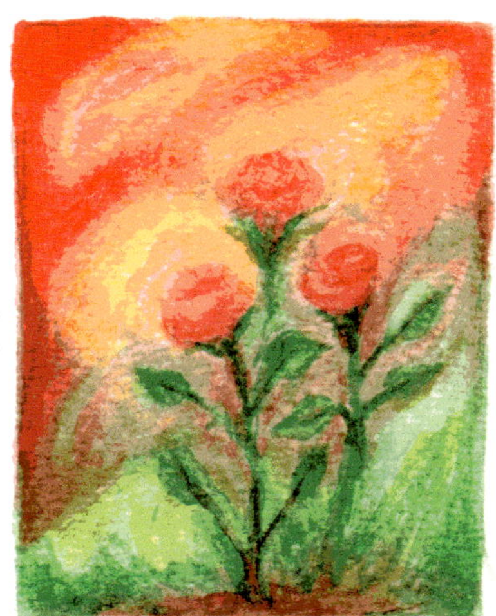

Fig. 12. *Roses* (author)

In Tao philosophy, the golden flower is the crystallisation of light and the attainment of immortality. Alchemical traditions see the blue flower as a symbol of the unattainable, the mysterious and the elusive – it was seen occasionally in dreams as a mystical inspiration leading the seeker onwards.

White flowers typify purity and innocence, such as the lily which is often included in paintings of the Annunciation. Red flowers, especially roses, are associated with love, both romantic and the higher aspects of sacrificial love; Christ's passion is symbolised by a rose, for example.

Mystics have been able to imaginatively penetrate the open cups of flowers, experiencing them as Grail Chalices receiving the divine light of the sun. The experience of flowers reflecting the inner soul-life, is referred to by Rudolf Steiner concerning a Rosicrucian path of spiritual training. He wrote,"The second stage of Rosicrucian training is imagination ... the full-blooming crocus becomes for us a visible image of a lonely being that strives upward in melancholy. The violet becomes a symbol for something that fulfils its existence in modest, calm beauty ... One flower becomes a tear through which the earth expresses its sorrow; another becomes an expression of joy."[1]

Similar imaginations lie behind the many interesting legends, myths and stories about the plant kingdom which give wonderfully rich and varied insights to the mysterious inter-relationships existing between people, events and plants. In mythology and legend we have the descriptions which once were the clearly perceived atavistic images of the true spirit-world, which lies behind the senses.

1. Rudolf Steiner, *The Christian Mystery*, pp. 141-2, quoted in 'Flower Essence Therapy and Rosicrucianism' by H. Reid Shaw, *New View* magazine.

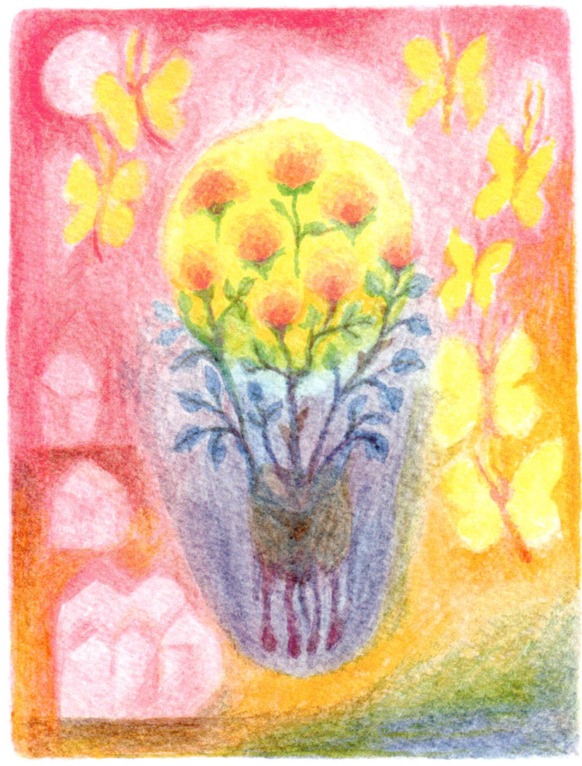

Fig 13. *The Rose as an Archetype* (author)

Each of nature's realms has its own distinct "place" within the spirit-worlds. As well as having its presence in the physical world, the plant realm exists also within the etheric realm. An individual with accurate sensitivity and a clear consciousness of the etheric realm can see the etheric archetypes, or imaginations lying behind the outer sense-world of nature. This was the everyday consciousness of the human being in ancient times, and as the clairvoyant faculties faded, this consciousness remained reachable in dream-states. Picture-images of nature's archetypes could be perceived through the sentient soul (that aspect of the soul which experiences perceptual sensations).

The sources of mythology are a combination of both the perceived spirit archetypes, and the reflected images of the soul's own spiritual experiences, especially that of the sentient soul, with its direct relationship to the forces and elements of nature.

References can be found in various lectures from Rudolf Steiner regarding such perceptions of the plant world.

In his lectures *The Apocalypse of St John* [2] he describes a clairvoyant condition in the following way: (paraphrased)

"The astral body of a person who practises certain occult exercises, gradually manifests many changes at night. Such exercises were given in the Oriental and Egyptian Mysteries, in the Pythagorean Schools, and are included in Rosicrucian meditative exercises based on the Gospel of St John.

"The main purpose of such exercises of meditation is to influence a person during the day, even if only for a short time, so that the effect continues when the person falls asleep and the astral body withdraws.

"The astral body gradually manifests different light-effects, and acquires an inner organisation such as the physical body possesses in its eyes, ears etc.

"When such inner astral organs have developed to a certain extent, the person begins to become conscious during sleep. A spiritual environment shines out of the otherwise universal darkness, and he perceives wonderful pictures of plant life. These are the most fundamental achievements of clairvoyance. Where previously there had been only the darkness of unconsciousness there now arises something of a dreamlike structure, yet living and real. Much of what is described in mythology was seen in this way. When we read in legends that Woden, Willy and Weh found a tree on the seashore and from that they created mankind, this indicates that it was first seen in such a dream-picture. In many mythologies you can perceive this fundamental kind of clairvoyant dream-sight, this vision of plants.

"Paradise is also the description of such a vision, with its two trees of knowledge and of life. It is the result of this astral vision. All that is described in the beginning of the Bible, in the book of Genesis, was seen in this manner. In former times, early Christians were told that 'Adam fell into a sleep', and that this was the sleep in which Adam, looking back, perceived the visions described in the book of Genesis."

In the next chapter we shall look at a variety of myths and legends which are to be found in almost every culture of the world. Some reflect the states of consciousness to which Steiner is referring; others embody the dreamlike memories of the inherited stream of mythology which has been passed down through many generations of oral tradition.

2. Twelve lectures given in Nuremberg, 17-30 June 1908. Lecture 2 (19 June 1908).

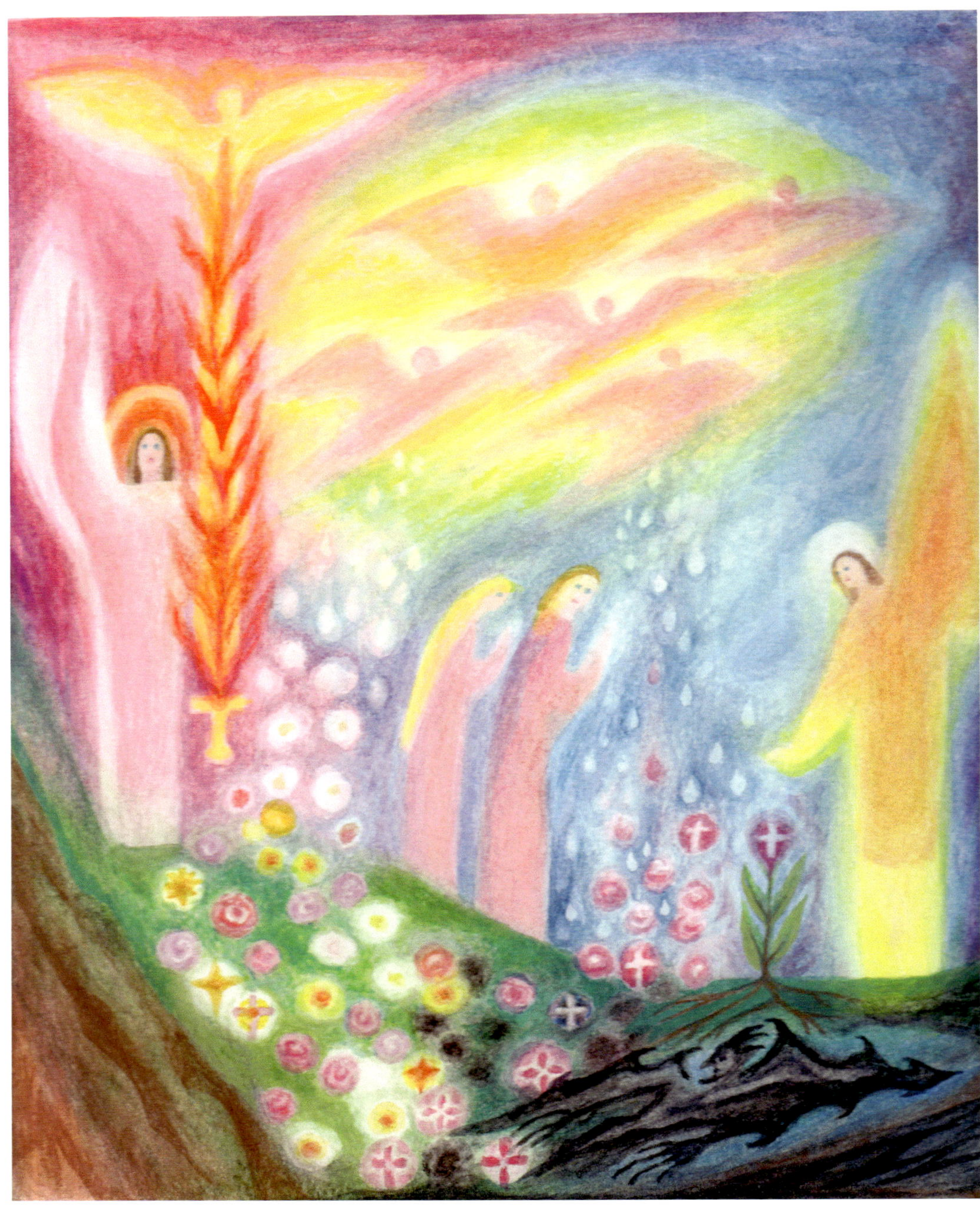

Fig 14. *Adam and Eve* (author). Legend: When Adam and Eve were expelled from Paradise, the tears of the Angels formed flowering plants. The Devil's spitting formed poisonous plants. The Archangel Raphael formed the sign of the cross on poisonous plants so that healers could use them as medicines.

CHAPTER TWO: MYTHS, LEGENDS AND TRADITIONS

> "I know a bank where the wild thyme blows,
> where oxlips and the nodding violet grows
> Quite over-canopied with luscious woodbine,
> with sweet musk-rose, and with eglantine ..."
>
> *A Midsummer Night's Dream*: Oberon, Act II, Sc. 1
> Shakespeare

Acanthus

Large-leafed perennial originating in the Mediterranean area. In Greek legend the sculptor Callimachus (fifth century BC) found the grave of a child. Upon it was a basket filled with her toys, covered with a terracotta tile. An acanthus plant had sprouted from the grave, its leaves curling around the sides of the basket. This inspired the Corinthian capital, which is a stylised basket wrapped in the scrolling leaves of the acanthus, a reference to new life emerging from the grave.

Alder

A tree or shrub from the birch family (*Betulaceae*), genus *Alnus*. In Norse mythology, the first human couple were created from the ash and the alder. Part of its mystical significance may be due to the fact that the wood turns from white to purple when it is cut, suggestive of blood. The alder is also a symbol of regeneration and resurrection, and is sacred in Ireland. In the Battle of the Trees, the gigantic Bran the Blessed was recognised by the alder branch he carried. Sacred to the god Cocidius, a Celtic hunter-god who signified the wild uncultivated aspects of nature.

Almond

In Christian art, the *mandorla* (Italian for almond) often surrounds illustrations of Christ. Traditionally it symbolises the womb, or a protective sheath. In Genesis (43:11) the almond is among "the best fruits in the land". When Aaron's rod blossomed, it bore almonds overnight. In folklore, Aaron's staff became represented by the magician's wand. After the Exodus from Egypt, Aaron's rod was placed with the rods of the other tribes in the tabernacle. It "budded and brought forth buds, and bloomed blossoms, and yielded almonds". (Numbers 17:8.) This signified that Yahweh had bestowed Aaron and his tribe of Levi, authority in the Hebrew priesthood.

In Moroccan Islamic legend, a princess named Hatim was turned into an almond tree. She belonged to the Tai tribe and was young, generous and open-hearted. Her father, angered by her generosity, and for distributing his wealth as well as her own, gave her a choice of exile or death. She chose death, but Allah, showing mercy upon her, rewarded her for her generosity and her kindness by turning her into a beautiful almond tree. Even today, as the almond tree she continues to distribute her gifts: flowers in the spring; sweet almonds to eat; nourishing pure oil. She inspires peace, and heals the troubled hearts of men.

In Chinese tradition, the almond tree represents feminine beauty, fortitude in sorrow and watchfulness. In Greek mythology, Phyllis, daughter of King Lycurgus and sister of Dryas, married Demophon (son of the hero Theseus), but she was loved by her brother, Acamas, with whom she had a son. Phyllis took her own life and was turned into an almond tree when Demophon did not return to her. Referred to in Ovid's *Heroides*, Book 2, and in Chaucer's *The Legend of Good Women*.

Amaethon

Celtic god of agriculture, son of Don, brother of Gwydion. He stole a dog, a lapwing and a roebuck from Arawn, god of the dead, which caused a war known as the Battle of the Trees (or the Battle of Cad Goddeu). In the war, Gwydion, turned all types of trees into fighting men. Amaethon and Gwydion, along with Llaw, defeated the underworld deities. The legend is described in the poem of Cad Goddeau in the *Book of Taliesin*. More recent scholars have taken the view that the poem represents a convoluted code of letters and learning based on runes, or the ancient Celtic tree-alphabet. It is thought that its message is connected to druidic magical practices.

Birch

Tree of the family *Betulaceae*, genus *Betula*. Beth, (meaning birch) is the first letter of the old Irish alphabet, and also symbolises the beginning of the new year. Birch leaves and birch elixir are used widely as medicinal teas and tonics, having a therapeutic effect on stiffness of joints, kidney stones, consumption and the healing of wounds. Brushes made of birch twigs have been used across Europe for centuries, as brooms and scourges. The birch tree grows under the influence of the planet Venus.

Bodhi Tree

Buddha gained his enlightenment under the Bodhi Tree. The tale of the tree is told in the Maha-Bodhi-Vamsa (the Great Bodhi Chronicle) written in the eleventh century, attributed to Upatissa. The tree is an example of the sacred fig or pipul, sacred to Hindus as a source of fertility, life and knowledge (or gnosis).

Blodeuedd

Celtic myth, whose name means "born of flowers". A beautiful woman, magically created from the blossoms of the oak, broom and meadowsweet by Math and Gwydion. She was the bride of Gwydion's nephew, Lleu, whose mother did not want him to marry a mere mortal woman. They lived happily together until one day, in Lleu's absence, Blodeuedd fell in love with Goronwy, the lord of Penllyn. They attempted to murder Lleu, who did not die but flew into the air in the shape of an eagle. Math and Gwydion avenged him by turning the beautiful enchanted Blodeuedd into an owl, the bird of the night.

Carnation

Fragrant herbaceous flower of the family *Caryophyllaceae*, genus *Dianthus*. In Christian lore, the carnation is said to have sprung from the tears of Mary on her way to the cross; in other versions, it appeared when Jesus was born.

Raphael's painting *The Madonna of the Pinks* shows the infant Jesus with his mother, holding carnations as a symbol of divine love and healing.[1]

Native Americans regarded the carnation as sacred to the dead, and place blooms around a body as preparation for burial. In Victorian flower language, the carnation represented "admiration". It is the symbol for Mother's Day in the USA. In secular painting it symbolises friendship and betrothal.

Cornflower

Bright blue flower (also pink or white) of the *Asteraceae* family, genus *Centaurea cyanus*. Its Latin name derives from Greek mythology: the centaur, Chiron, healed a wound poisoned by the Hydra's blood by covering it with petals from the flower. Cyanus was a Greek youth who was lovesick for Chloris (or Flora). He spent his time gathering the blooms to place on her altars, and after his death she transformed him into the flower. (Cyan is also the name of a blue colour, after the Greek *kuanos*, a blue mineral.) Cornflowers often grew in fields of grain.

1. In the National Gallery, London.

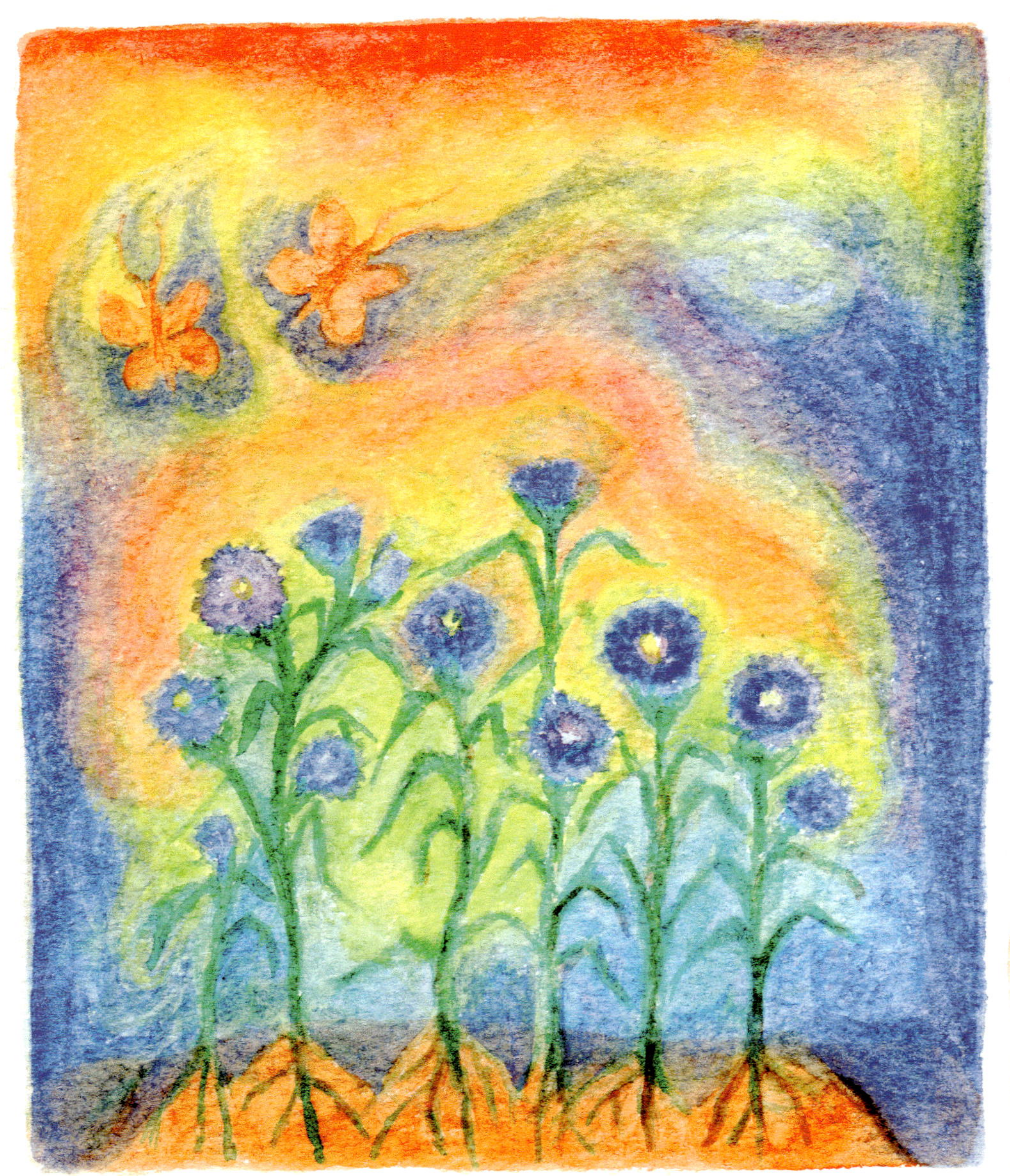

Fig. 15. *Cornflower* (author)

Daphne

Daughter of the Greek-river god, Peneus. She was a virgin huntress who happily and freely roamed the forests. One day Eros shot arrows at Apollo, who fell immediately in love with Daphne and pursued her. On the banks of her father's river she prayed desperately for help, and was changed into a laurel tree.

Date Palm

Fruit-bearing tree, *Arecaceae* or Palma, genus *Phoenix dactylifera*. Its name is derived from the belief that the tree will regrow itself, like the Phoenix bird, if it is destroyed. Grows throughout the Middle East, Africa and California. Its root is medicinal; the wood is used for building; the juice for wine; the seeds can be ground into oil; the leaves are woven into furniture and baskets; the fibre into rope; and the fruit is delicious for eating. In ancient Egypt and China the date palm was the tree of life. In Christian lore, Mary rests under this tree, and it is often depicted in paintings of the Holy Family on their journey to Egypt.

St Dorothy

Third century Christian patron saint of brewers, brides, florists, gardeners, newly-weds and midwives. Her life is outlined in *The Golden Legend,* a collection of saints' lives, written by Jacobus de Voragine in the thirteenth century. Just before she was martyred by the Governor of Caesarea, a young lawyer, Theophilus mocked her, saying "Send me fruit and flowers from that garden of paradise where you claim to be going to meet your bridegroom!" St Dorothy replied that his request would be fulfilled.

As she was dying, an angel, or the Christ child, appeared with a basket of three apples and three roses. When St Dorothy asked, he took them to Theophilus. He became a Christian but was later also martyred. In Christian art St Dorothy is depicted with the Christ child, and a basket of fruit and flowers.

Dryads

Greek wood nymphs who lived in trees, dying when the tree died. Crowned with oak-leaves, sometimes armed with an axe to punish outrages against the trees which they guarded, they would dance around the oaks which were sacred to them. Referred to in Pope's *Moral Essays* and Keats' *Ode to a Nightingale.*

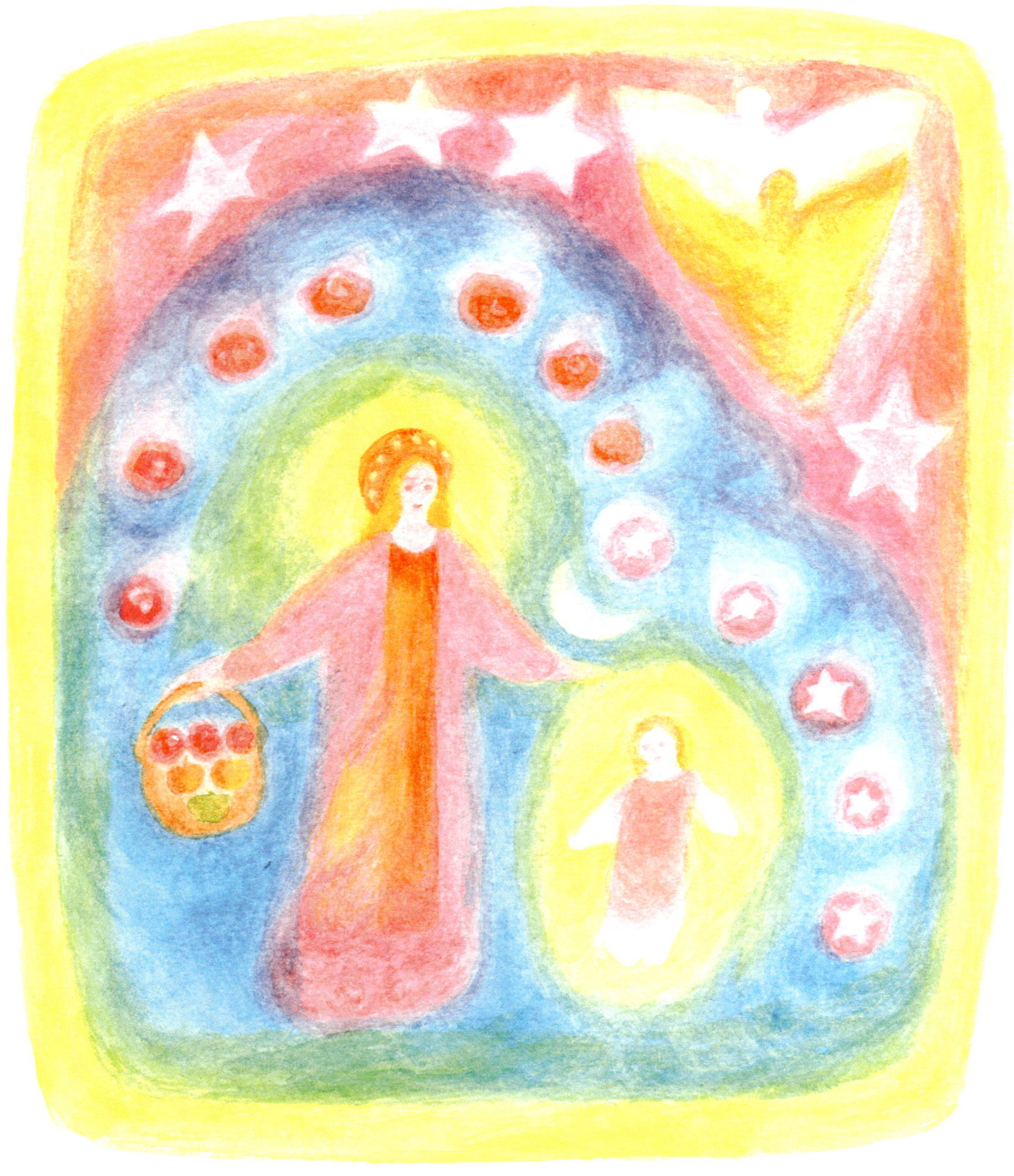

Fig. 16. St Dorothy (author)

Fig

Fruit tree of the *Moraceae* family (the mulberry), genus *Ficus*. One of the earliest trees to be cultivated, it has been a staple food of many cultures in Asia, Africa and Mediterranean Europe since ancient times. It is a symbol for prosperity and plenty, as well as having a variety of symbolic means in different cultures. The Romans regarded the fig tree as sacred to Dionysos; in Islamic tradition it is sacred because Muhammad gave his word on it; Buddha found enlightenment beneath the pipul tree, which is a type of fig. Adam and Eve clothed themselves with fig leaves on seeing their nakedness in the Garden of Eden. In some traditions the fig, not the apple, was the forbidden fruit. In Sicilian folklore Judas Iscariot hanged himself on a fig tree, but contrastingly, in Estonia, it is said that Jesus once sheltered from the rain beneath a fig tree, which he rewarded by bestowing it evergreen foliage.

The fig tree is also mentioned in the Gospel of St. John (John 1: 45)

"Jesus saw Nathanael coming to him and said of him 'behold an Israelite indeed, in whom is no guile!' Nathanael said unto him 'Whence knowest thou me?' Jesus answered, 'I saw thee before thou come to me: before Philip called thee, when you were under the fig tree, I saw thee.' Nathanael answered and said to him 'Rabbi, thou art the Son of God, thou art the King of Israel.' Jesus answered 'Because I said unto thee "I saw thee under the fig tree" believest thou? You shall see greater things than these. Verily, verily I say unto you: hereafter you shall see the heavens open and the angels of God ascending and descending upon the Son of Man'."

How can we understand this reference to the fig tree and its significance? The term is used in the same sense as in connection with the Buddha: the fig tree is the Bodhi tree, a symbol of initiation. Christ is saying to Nathanael that he sees him clairvoyantly as being an initiate of the fifth degree, which bears the name of the people to whom he belongs (eg. an Israelite, a Persian). "An Israelite in whom the truth dwells." Here there is no mere allegorical reference to the fig tree, but an expression alluding to an initiation of a high degree.

Fir

In Phrygia the pine tree was sacred to Cybele, and in ancient Roman mythology, Rhea turned Attis into a pine tree to prevent his death.

The Romans regarded unopened pine cones as symbols of virginity, and were sacred to Diana. The pine was one of Dionysos' sacred trees, whose followers often wore foliage from the fir tree.

One Yakut shamanic legend holds that the souls of the great shamans were found in the highest branches of the fir tree, and lesser shamans on the lower branches. Shamans regarded the fir as being the Universal Tree which grows symbolically in

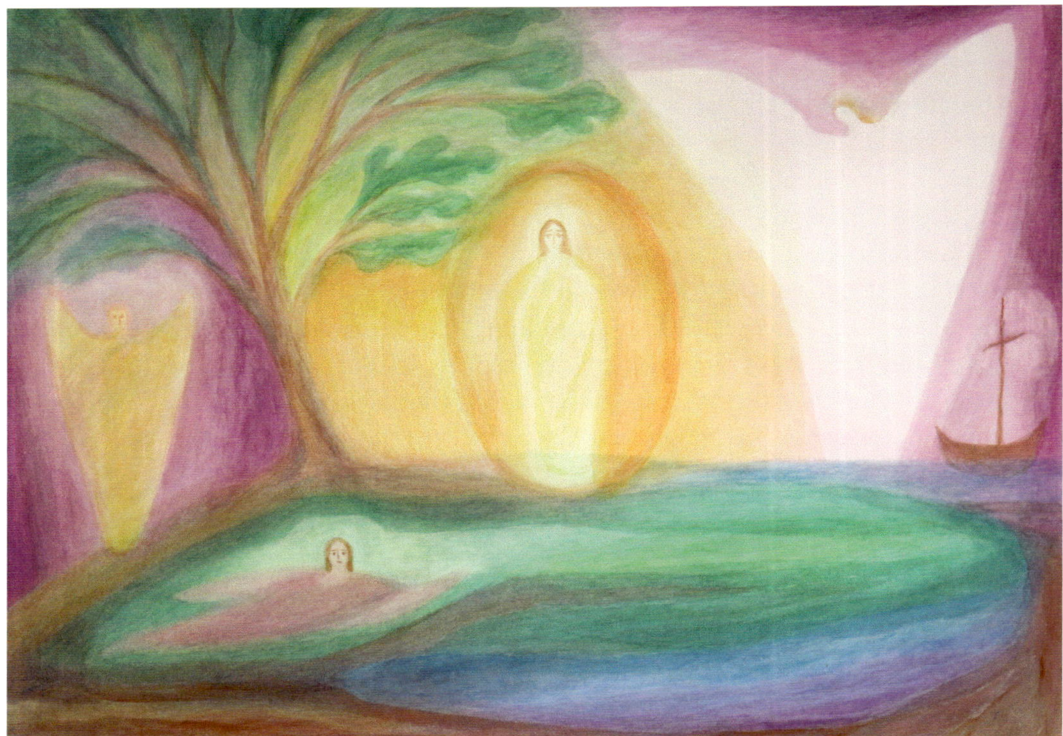

Fig. 17. *Nathanael under the fig tree*

the centre of the world. It was known as the axis of the world – the Axis Mundi – which spans the different worlds, and allows the mystic to access one plane of reality to another. It served as a symbolic bridge between everyday existence and the supernatural or super-sensible dimension.

<u>Fleur-de-lis</u>

Heraldic emblem, which is particularly associated with the French royal arms. The fleur-de-lis is a stylised representation of a lily, which traditionally symbolises purity. A French legend tells how Clovis, King of the Franks (466-511 AD) received a lily from heaven at his baptism. From the time of Louis VIII, golden lilies on a blue background were established as the royal arms, and in 1376 Charles V decreed that there should be only three fleurs-de-lis, in honour of the Holy Trinity.

<u>Hazel</u>

Tree of the birch family. In Norse mythology the hazel tree is sacred to Thor the thunder-god, and is believed to be the actual embodiment of lightning. A medieval German legend says that Herodias, the wife of King Herod who had John the Baptist beheaded, was in love with the prophet. When his head was brought to her on the platter she tried to kiss it, but it drew back and blew hard at her. Herodias was whirled up to the top of a hazel tree, where she still sits from midnight to cock crow, floating in the air the rest of the time. Medieval German Christians would place hazel twigs in the form of a cross on their windowsills during a storm, in the hope of stilling it. In European folklore it was the custom for the leader of a wedding-party to carry a hazel wand, to ensure many offspring for the marriage.

Heliades

From Ovid's *Metamorphoses*, Book 2, comes the legend of the Heliades, the three daughters of Apollo and Clymene, whose names were Aegiale, Aegle and Aetheria. When their brother Phaethon died, they grieved so much that they were transformed into poplar trees.

Another legend goes as follows: Phaethon pleaded with his father Apollo to let him drive his chariot. Apollo finally relented, but Phaethon could not control it. The chariot plunged down to the earth and parched Libya. Zeus, in return, killed the boy with a thunderbolt. Phaethon fell into the Eridanus, or Po river, and was transformed into a swan. There his three sisters, the Heliades, mourning him, were turned into willow trees and their tears into drops of amber.

Hyacinth

A fragrant flower of the lily family growing annually in spring, from a large bulb. In Greek mythology the hyacinth is associated with the love which the god Apollo had for the young boy Hyacinthus. The god of the wind, Zephyr, was also in love with Hyacinthus and killed him with a discus, sent on the wind. Hyacinthus' blood was turned into a flower and Apollo declared an annual three-day festival, Hyacinthia, in his honour. Sacrifices were offered to the dead youth and his sad fate was recounted in songs, on the first and third days. On the second day, hymns to Apollo were sung, joy and socialising reigned, as citizens kept open house for friends and relatives.

Another account holds that the flower bloomed from the blood of the hero Ajax, when he lost a fighting contest with Odysseus.

In Christian symbolism the hyacinth signifies prudence, peace of mind, and an aspiration towards heaven.

Iris

Highly prized and regarded as sacred due to its majestic uprightness and large complex bloom. Often depicted as the flower of the Virgin Mary in early works of art, denoting purity. In traditional Spanish and Netherlandish painting, the iris is associated with the immaculate conception.

<u>Ivy</u>

Evergreen vine belonging to the *Araliaceae* family, genus *Hedera*. In Greek mythology, ivy was sacred to Dionysos. It was said that the god was so moved by a worshipper who danced herself to death before him, that he transformed her body into ivy, which embraces its support. Dionysos wears a garland-crown of ivy, and the vine was considered to be a charm against inebriation. In Christian lore the evergreen ivy symbolises eternal life, and is often used in church decoration, for example, on baptismal fonts, and in border designs of illuminated manuscripts.

<u>Larkspur</u>

Herbaceous plant of the buttercup (*Ranunculaceae*) family, genus *Delphinium*. The Greek name, Delphinium, related this plant to a dolphin because of the shape of the nectary. Its common name larkspur, derives from the resemblance of the flower to larks' claws.

The larkspur was said to have sprung from the blood of Ajax, the Greek hero who died at Troy. The Romans considered the flower to have once been a dolphin, transformed by Neptune to save it from being caught by fishermen. An Italian tradition claims that it grew out of dragons' blood, because of its being blue and poisonous.

<u>Lily</u>

The *Lilium Candidum*, symbol of purity associated particularly with the Virgin Mary and the virgin saints. It features in the Annunciation, placed in a vase or growing in a pot, or held in the hand of the Archangel Gabriel, becoming the symbol of the incarnation. Medieval theologians held that the Annunciation took place in the springtime, inspiring St Bernard to write of Christ: "The flower willed to be born of a flower, in a flower, at the time of flowers."

Among the female saints, the lily belongs especially to Catherine of Siena; Clare; Euphemia and Scolastica. The Christ sitting in judgement is sometimes depicted with a lily and a sword on either side.

The lily was also adapted into the symbol of the fleur-de-lis, which is the emblem of the French kings. According to legend, Clovis chose it as the emblem of his purification by baptism when he became Christian. It was adopted by the monarchy in the twelfth century. Charlemagne wore it on his ermine cloak; Louis IX on his cloak; and Louis of Toulouse on his cape. It was the insignia of Florence, and is thus also the emblem of the bishop Zenobius. St Anthony of Padua (Italy) is also depicted with the lily as his token.

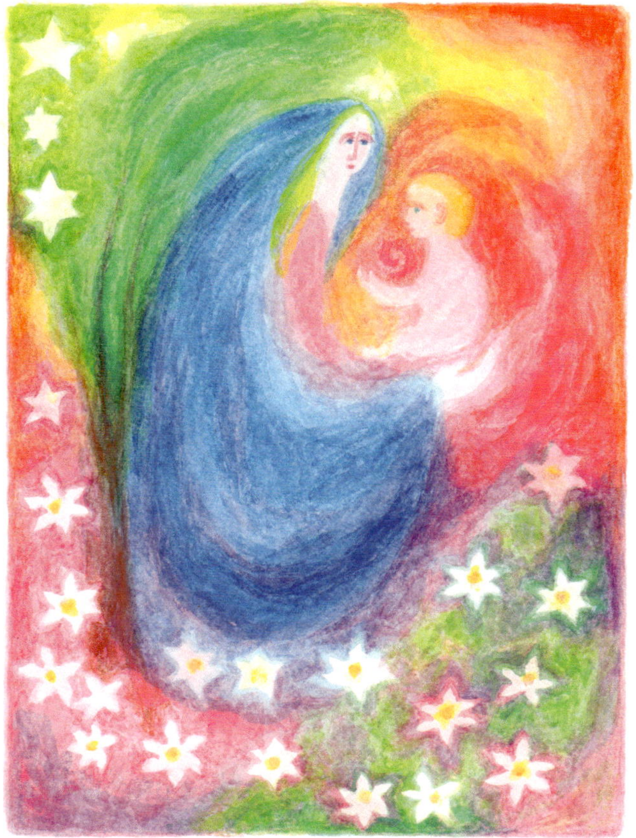 Fig. 18. Lily-lady (author)

An anonymous poem from the Middle Ages reads:

> O Lily-lady
> Dreaming serenely alone in cloud-garden shady,
> No longer mayst thou muse, no more repose
> O Lily-lady
> In thy garden shady.
>
> The great rose
> Now waking, his crimson splendour doth loftily dispose;
> Now is thy calm day done, now the star-daisies close,
> O Lily-lady
> In thy garden shady. [1]

1. Quoted in *The Spirit of Man* by Robert Bridges.

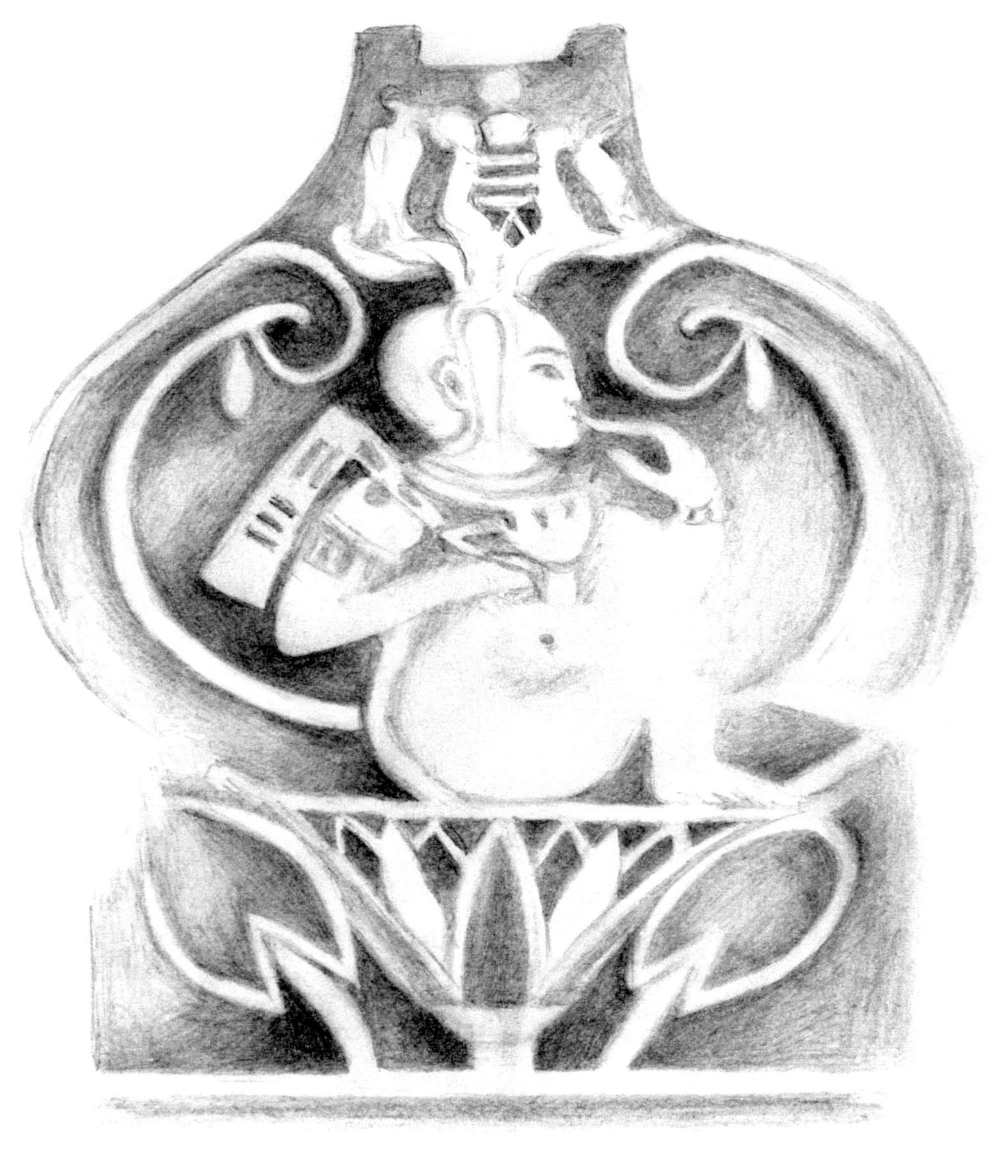

Fig. 19. Ivory in Egyptian style depicting the god Horus as an infant child seated on a lotus flower, from the palace at Samaria, ninth century BC (author's drawing)

<u>Lotus</u>

A flowering plant, sacred in many cultures. In ancient Egypt it was dedicated to the sun-god Horus, who had come forth out of the lotus blossom, thereby gaining eternal youth. In ancient Persia it was regarded as a symbol of the sun.

In Hindu tradition the lotus flower represents the procreation of life, and the earth goddess, source of all creation. It is also sacred because Brahma was born from it. The lotus heralded the birth of Gautama Buddha, and lotus flowers sprang up in the Buddha's footprints. The Bodhisattva is often depicted seated on a lotus flower throne.

In Chinese Buddhism, the Western Heaven is the location of the Sacred Lake of Lotuses. Here the souls of the virtuous rest in lotus buds and when the lotus opens, the soul is released into the presence of the god of paradise.

Spiritual organs of the human being known as chakras, have a lotus shape, the petals of which are opened or set into motion, as each stage of spiritual development is attained.

<u>May Day</u>

This is an ancient European fertility celebration and ritual which has survived as a spring festival. It began in pre-Christian times as part of the agricultural rituals celebrating the new life-forces of the springtime, of winter being overcome, and the warmth and light of the sun returning. In the ancient Scandinavian festival, mock battles were staged to represent the annual battle between winter and summer.

Traditional May Day festivities include elaborate interweaving dances around a maypole, as long colourful ribbons are intertwined by the dancers. This might have originated in the clairvoyant perceptions of the interweaving etheric life-forces of the trees in the spring. Dancing and rejoicing with colourful decorations, wreaths of flowers and traditional white costumes, May Day celebrants share in nature's jubilation.

Some customs chose a man or a boy to be dressed from head-to-foot in greenery, as representative of the vegetative nature spirit. He would lead a procession, symbolising the return of the god of growth. Others chose a young maiden to be crowned with fresh flowers as the May Queen.

<u>Myrrh</u>

A tree resin used for incense. In Greek mythology there was once a princess, Myrrha, who was in love with her father, Cinyras, King of Cyprus. In her shame she attempted suicide, but her nurse helped her by arranging a tryst with her father, ensuring that he was drunk with wine. After several encounters he discovered that his mistress was his own daughter, and horrified by his incest, tried to kill her. Myrrha fled to the land of Sabaea where she gave birth to a son, Adonis. She then turned into a tree, the myrrh. Adonis was worshipped with the burning of myrrh incense at his festival.

In Christian tradition myrrh was one of the gifts which the three Wise Men, or Magi, brought from the East to the new-born Christ-child.

Myrtle

An evergreen shrub. In Greece, myrtle was sacred to Aphrodite and associated with birth and resurrection. Greek colonists carried myrtle boughs to their new countries to symbolise the end of one life and the beginning of another.

In Roman custom, myrtle was sacred to Venus, and was a symbol of love and marriage, where both Venus and Juno presided. Brides wore myrtle blossoms and bridegrooms wore leafy sprigs.

Narcissus

Bulbous flowering plant of the *Amaryllis* family, genus *Narcissus*. In Greek mythology, Narcissus was the beautiful son of Cephissus and Liriope. He rejected the advances of the nymph, Echo, who pined away for love until nothing was left but her voice. When he saw his own reflection in a pool, Narcissus fell in love with it eventually dying of frustrated desire, a punishment of the gods for his rejecting Echo. The plant grew up from his body.

Oak Tree

Large enduring tree of the genus *Quercus* (family *Fagaceae*), having many ancient mythical and magical associations. In both Greek and Roman tradition the first food of mankind was the acorn. North American Indians, who ate acorns, believed the oak was a gift from Wy-ot, the firstborn of the sky and the earth.

An oracle to Zeus in Dodona, north-eastern Greece, was located in an oak-grove, where the priestesses pronounced oracles after listening to the rustling of the oak leaves. Worshippers of the Phoenician god, Baal, made sacrificial offerings "under every leafy oak". (Ezekial 6:13)

The oak was sacred to the Roman god Jove, or Jupiter; and was later held sacred in Scandinavia to Thor, where it was known as "the thunder tree". It was highly regarded by the Jews because Abraham had encountered an angel of Jehovah beneath its branches.

Worshipped by the Druids, whose magical rites were conducted using oak and mistletoe, even Merlin was said to have performed his magic under its shelter. In

Germany, when St Boniface wanted to convert the populace, one of his first acts was to destroy an oak tree sacred to the Druids.

In Christmas celebrations of Northern Europe, oak became the traditional wood for the Yule log. The oak grows under the influence of Mars.

<u>Pansy</u>

A species of violet, most commonly the wild pansy (Viola tricolor, of the family *Violaceae*). In Scottish and German folklore it is known as Stepmother, or Stiefmütterchen; the largest central petal is the stepmother with her two richly coloured daughters beside her, while the two pale petals above them are her stepdaughters.

In a Romanian legend, the pansy was once a beautiful servant-girl in the royal court, with whom a prince had fallen in love. The jealous queen wished that she would turn into a toad and tried to cast a spell on her. However, her nature was so lovely that she instead changed into a pansy.

In Shakespeare's *Midsummer Night's Dream*, Puck squeezes the juice of a pansy plant into Titania's eyes to make her fall in love with the first creature she sees.

<u>Pomegranate</u>

A fruit bearing many seeds, *Punica granatum* (family *Punicaceae*), cultivated since ancient times. Traditionally associated with Adam and Eve, who, disobeying God's instructions, ate one growing on the Tree of Knowledge in the Garden of Eden.

The Phrygian god of death and resurrection, Attis, was said to have been conceived when his virgin-mother, Nana, laid a pomegranate on her breast. (Attis was later changed into a pine tree, and is known as the god of vegetation.)

In Greek mythology Persephone is obliged to spend four months every year in Hades because she ate four pomegranate seeds.

The pomegranate was recommended by the Prophet Muhammad to cleanse oneself from hatred and envy. In Christian tradition, the pomegranate is also regarded as a symbol of hope. Zoroastrians in Persia used branches from the pomegranate tree as a protective charm. In Sicily its branches are used in dowsing, and in Spain the fruit is the national emblem.

<u>Poppy</u>

Brightly coloured flower of the family *Papaveraceae*, genus *Papaver*. In Greek mythology Demeter was granted sleep by smelling a poppy sent by the gods, when she roamed exhausted in her search for Persephone. Traditionally the poppy, (from which opium is derived) has been used for pain relief and recreational smoking, which induces a dreamy other-worldly trance.

In Christian lore the red poppy is said to have sprung up from the blood of the crucified Christ. Himalayan cultivation has produced the rare brilliant-blue poppy.

Wheat fields bear scarlet poppies with the grain, and the poppy has become an emblem of remembrance for those who lost their lives in the World Wars.

<u>Poplar</u>

Tree of the family *Salicaceae*, genus *Populus*. In Roman mythology when Hercules visited the underworld he wore a crown of poplar. The upper side of the leaves were scorched and darkened by the heat; the undersides became radiantly silver from the sweat of the hero. Perhaps originating from Hercules' successful return from the underworld, the poplar has become a symbol for life after death.

In the Irish tree-alphabet, the white poplar represented old age and autumn.

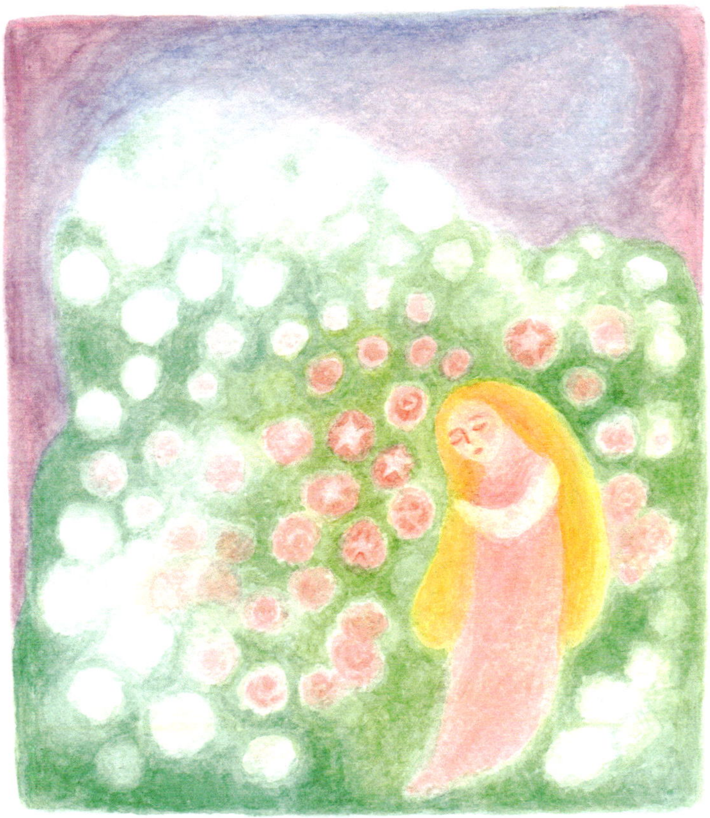

Fig. 20. *Eve kissing roses in Eden* (author)

<u>Rose</u>

Family *Rosaceae*, genus *Rosa*. A thorny shrub renowned for its beautiful fragrant flowers and having a world-wide folklore, symbolising death and resurrection; beauty; secrecy; suffering and love.

The rose is said to have grown in the Garden of Eden. It was originally white but blushed pink when Eve kissed its petals. An early Christian legend claims that before the Fall, the rose had no thorns; in later Christian tradition Christ was symbolised by an image of a rose without thorns.

In western tradition the rose is associated with feminine beauty and purity. The Virgin Mary is often symbolised by a rose, which also signified love incarnate. The Christian esoteric stream, the Rosicrucians, have the Rose-Cross as their symbol.

In Greek mythology the rose became red from the blood of Venus, whose feet were pricked by its thorns as she sought Adonis. Another legend tells how Cupid shot an arrow into the rose after being stung by a bee when he bent to smell the flower, hence its sharp thorns. Cupid was also said to have mischievously poured a cup of wine over the flower, staining it red.

The colour red was also attributed to the divine blood of Christ, when he was crowned with the crown of thorns made from branches of the rose bush.

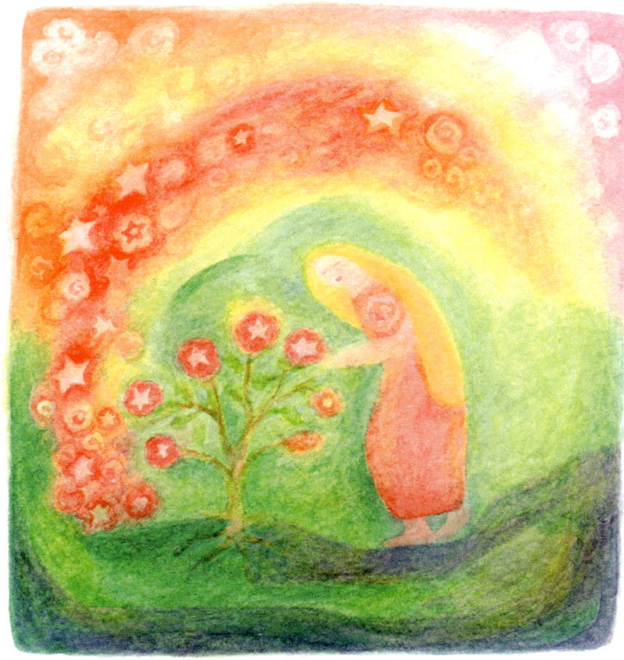

Fig 21. *Eve in the Garden of Eden* (author)

Roses are also associated with miracles. When Zoroaster was placed into the fire as a baby, he was unharmed, as the flames turned into roses. Legends also relate that flames, which burned several martyrs, were afterwards transformed into red roses.

The white rose was said to have sprung from the tears of Muhammad on his journey from heaven. Legend holds that the rose, originating from India, was brought to the west by Alexander the Great. Even during the Napoleonic Wars, couriers were given special protection and dispensation to bring back rare rose species for the extensive gardens of the Empress Josephine at Malmaison.

From classical times until the present, the rose has been associated with death and resurrection. Rose bushes have been planted on graves since Roman times, and during the Rosalia festivals rose petals were strewn onto the graves. Today they continue to serve as memorials for loved ones throughout the world.

Many fairytales and legends feature roses. The nightingale was so enamoured of the rose that it pierced its breast on the thorns, staining the rose red with blood. Sleeping Beauty's castle was surrounded with thickets of thorns, which parted and blossomed when her prince arrived. Beauty came to live with the Beast in his castle, as forfeit for her request for a rose, which her father had plucked from the Beast's garden.

<u>Shen Nung – Divine Farmer</u>

Chinese culture hero, the ox-headed divine farmer, second of the Five Sovereigns. He taught men the art of agriculture, the healing use of plants, medicines and drugs. He is also honoured as a god of medicine, and the god of burning wind.

<u>Silvanus</u>

Roman god of agriculture who watches over hunters, shepherds and boundaries. Silvanus also protected parks and gardens. Roman art portrayed him as a strong woods-man. Virgil's *Aeneid*, Book 8, describes a grove near Caere, dedicated to Silvanus, which served as a boundary between Latium and Etruria. Originally the Celtic god Cocidius.

<u>The Tree of Life</u>

In the Kabbalah, the multiple symbol known in Hebrew as the Otz Chiim. The Tree consists of ten spheres or sephiroth, out of which, according to mystical tradition, the creation of the world came about.

The ten sephiroth are aligned in three columns headed by the supernals: Kether, Chokhmah and Binah. Together these symbolise the process by which the Infinite Light, Ain Soph Aur, becomes manifest in the Universe. Beneath the supernals are the "seven days of creation": Chesed, Gevurah, Tiferet, Netzach, Hod, Yesod and Malchut. Taken as a whole the Tree of Life is also a symbol of the archetypal human being, Adam Kadmon. The mystical path of self-knowledge involves the unfolding of all the levels of one's own being, from Malchut (physical reality) to the infinite Source.

Thistle

Prickly weed, common species of *Carduus* and *Cirsium* of the family *Asteraceae*. The thistle is associated with the Virgin Mary; the sacred thistle (*Carduus benedictus*) is said to have grown from a nail from Christ's cross which Mary had planted into the ground.

It is the national emblem of Scotland, from a tradition that in the mid-tenth century a bare-footed raiding party of Danes attempting to attack Staines Castle by night, were thwarted by the thistles growing in the dry moat. In 1687, James VII of Scotland and II of England, established a chivalric brotherhood of Scottish knights known as the Order of the Thistle. A medieval French order also named the Order of the Thistle was founded in honour of the Virgin Mary.

Violet

Small flowering plant, genus *Viola*, family *Violaceae*, with purple, violet or blue petals and a delicate fragrance.

In Greek mythology the violet is said to have sprung from the blood of Attis, or to have been created by Zeus to feed Io, whom he had transformed into a cow.

In Christian tradition the shadow of Christ on the cross fell over the violet, causing it to hang its head and to droop. It is also considered to be sacred to the Virgin Mary being associated with humility, suffering and mourning.

Its sweet perfume is both soothing and comforting.

Yggdrasil

The great world-tree in Norse mythology, and known as the Cosmic Ash in Germanic lore. Yggdrasil lay at the heart of the Universe. It is the largest tree ever to have grown; its branches overhang the nine worlds of the Norsemen and spread out above the heavens. It was supported by three great roots; one descended into Jotunheim, the land of the giants, the second root grew into misty Niflheim; the third reached Asgard, the dwelling place of the gods.

Odin hung himself on Yggdrasil for nine nights as an initiation to learn wisdom. A parallel with Christ's crucifixion can be drawn, as Odin was also pierced with a spear and cried out before he died.

The idea of a cosmic tree is common in the myths of Northern Europe and Asia.

In Ireland the branches became magical and musical, made of silver or gold, and brought by messengers from other-world lands.

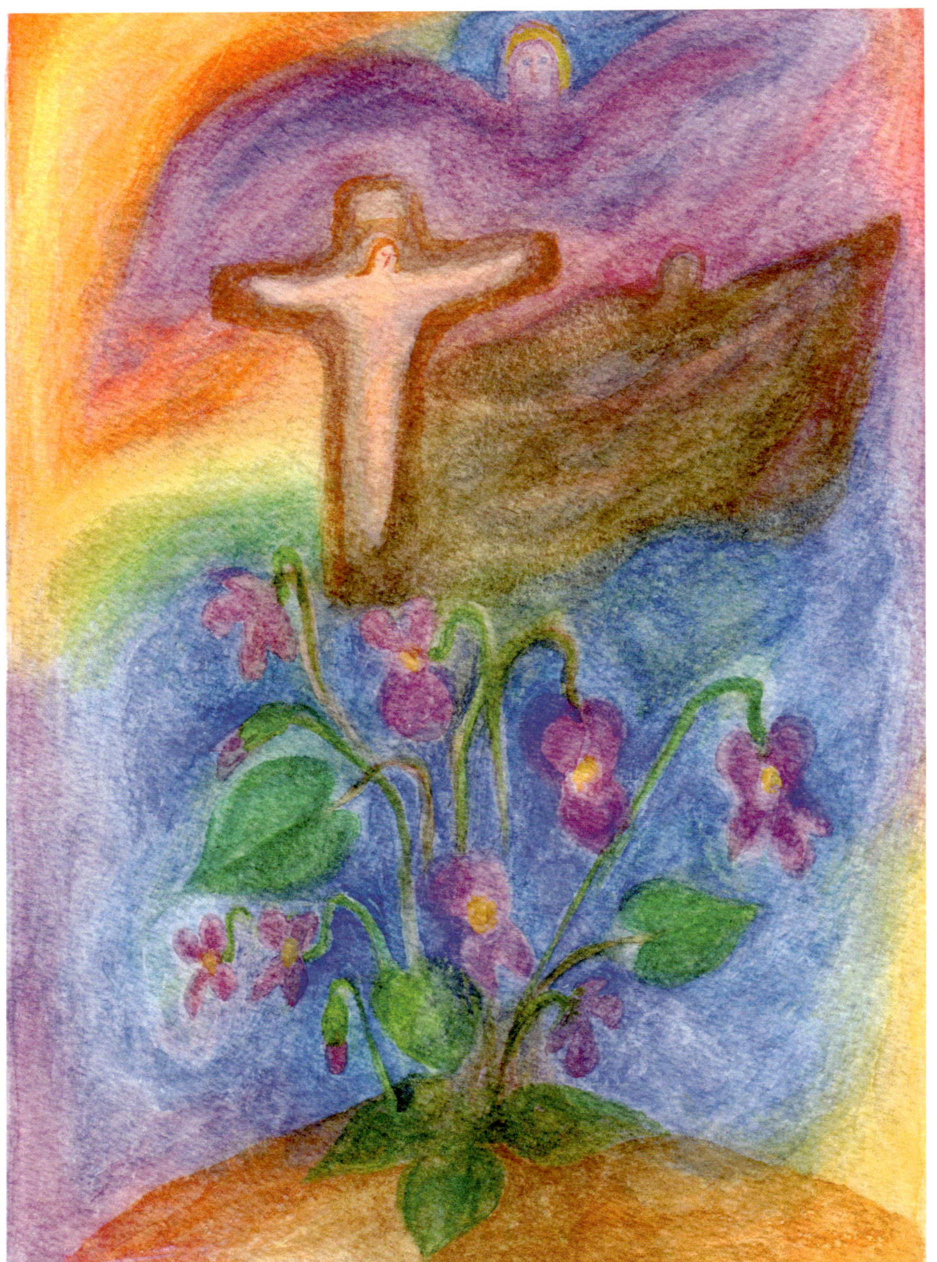

Fig. 22. *Violet at the Crucifixion* (author)

PART THREE

CHAPTER ONE: INFLUENCES FROM THE COSMOS

All things by immortal power
Near or far
Hiddenly
To each other linkèd are,
That thou canst not stir a flower
Without troubling of a star ...

Francis Thompson, 'The Mistress of Vision'

Knowledge of the relationships between heaven and earth has only relatively recently in the evolution of humanity, been lost to the intellectual rationalism of modern science. In the past, both the faculties of natural clairvoyance and a healthy moral sensitivity towards nature and the cosmos, meant that the interconnectedness of heavenly and earthly matters was intimately experienced.

Various traditions linked plants, herbs and trees with the planets and the zodiac. Theophrastus Paracelsus (1493-1541) wrote:

"You should know that every star in the sky is nothing other than a herb grown in the spirit ... every star begets through its formative power a kindred herb on the earth...

"And so every herb is an earthly star and looks upwards towards the heavens, and every star is a celestial herb ... looking down to the earth, to the herbs which they have begotten. If you knew the link you would say:

"This star is called Stella Rosmarini, the Star of Rosemary; this one is called Stella Absythii, the Star of Absinth – Artemesia Absinthia ..."[1]

Agrippa of Nettesheim (1486-1535) wrote:

"Also amongst vegetation, everything that bears fruit is from Jupiter, and everything that bears flowers is from Venus; all seed and bark is from Mercury; and all roots from Saturn; and all wood from Mars, all leaves from the Moon. Wherefore all that bring forth fruit and flowers are of Saturn and Jupiter, but they that bring forth flowers and seed and not fruit are from Venus and Mercury; these which are brought forth of their own accord without seed are of the Moon and Saturn; all beauty is from Venus; all strength is from Mars; and every planet rules, and disposeth that which is like to it".[2]

1. Quoted in *The Golden Blade,* 1988: *Seven Trees and Seven Planets* by Johannes Hemleben.
2. Agrippa of Nettesheim, Chapter 30 of Book 1, *The Three Books of Occult Philosophy.*

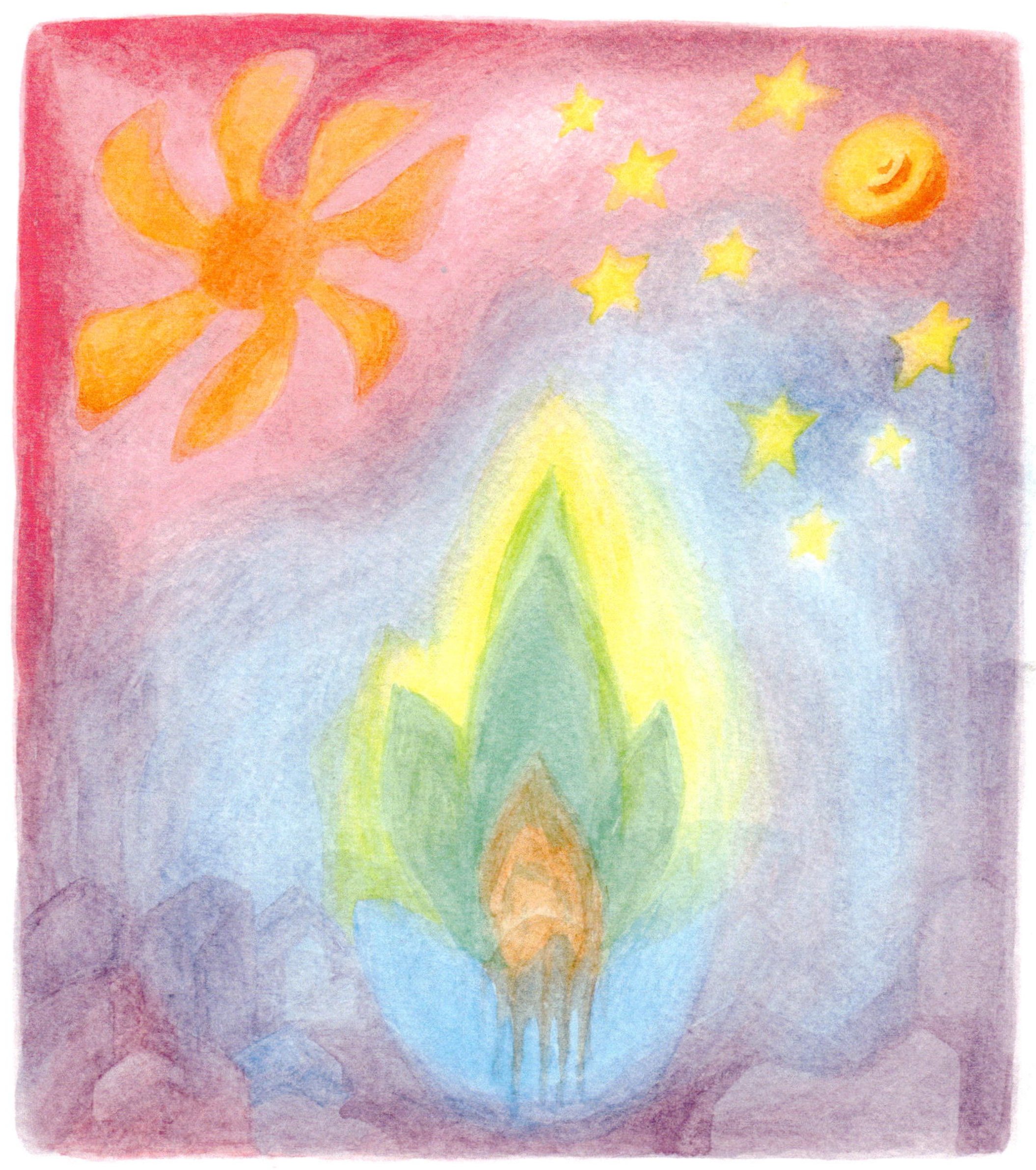

Fig. 23. *Plant with Sun and Moon* (author)

The Divine Mind

The mystical philosopher Bernard Silvestris wrote

"... for anything which is brought forth to assume the mode of being proper to its kind derives the cause and nature of its substantial existence from the celestial sphere, as though from a life giving god. For how are the stars borne about in a ceaseless journey, if not because they have imbided ethereal nourishment? How would the creatures of the land, the waters, the air, move if they had not received enlivening impulses from the firmament? ...

"When the vital spirit of life has been summoned from the vault of heaven, earth applies herself to providing nurture for bodily existences, and does not cease from the task of nourishment until she has ensured a sufficiency of created natures ... This is the wisdom of God, conceived and nourished by the living fountains of eternity. From this wisdom arises the deliberation, from deliberation the will, and from the divine will the shaping of cosmic life ...

"The great lights, the sun and moon and all the wandering spheres, whose circling never ceases, do not suffer the elements of the underlying world to remain unmoving. This elementing nature is in fact the firmament, and those stars which traverse the circle of the zodiac arouse the elements to their natural activity ...

"The life and well-being of the universe depend on sovereign and ancient causes: spirit, sentience, a source of motivation and a source of order. The divine exemplars live eternal; without their life the visible creation would not live everlastingly ... Many things spring from the earth, but without the stimulus of a principle of growth, neither tree nor shoot nor anything else would thrive. Thus from the life of the divine mind, from the spirit, from the world soul, from the growth principle of created life, the eternity of the universe has its rise ... the firmament learns from the divine mind, the stars from the firmament and the universe from the stars, whence their life derives and how they may discern the course of existence ... From the mind-universe the sense-universe was born, perfect from perfect."[3]

3. Bernadus Silvestrus, *Cosmographia.*

Venus

The planet Venus has particular associations with plants, especially from ancient Greek times when it was accepted that the plants sacred to Venus were the rose and the myrtle. The planet Venus, depending on its position relative to the Sun, can be both a morning and evening star. When it follows the Sun and is an evening star in the western sky, it is called Hesperus (of the West); when it precedes the Sun and appears before sunrise in the East, it is called Lucifer (light-bringing). Thus, the rose of Lucifer was dedicated to Venus, also the myrtle tree of Hesperus.

In his lectures *The Influence of Spiritual Beings Upon Man*, Rudolf Steiner spoke about the planet Venus in the following way: (paraphrased)

"Venus is connected in a certain way through its forces, with our whole earthly vegetation and all that lives on earth. This has an effect on us through our nourishment. Influences of the Venus beings live in all the plants, and in the animals. We absorb these beings into our bodies. Certain plants flourish in certain countries, under celestial influences. This gives rise to particular national characteristics. Folk character can be formed in this way, from the spiritual beings which are absorbed into the human being with his food."[4]

The Staff of Mercury

Goethe envisioned the organs, or different parts of a plant, as being arranged around a "spiritual staff". He spoke of the law-giving power in their midst, within the central axis of the vegetative part of the plant. This region is usually hollow, or contains only pith, and is surrounded outwardly by the stalk or stems. Goethe also saw the staff containing an "infinite within", and having an ethereal inner space – it was not a physical or material staff. It was the line followed by "the star of life", as it drew the plant forms forth. Along it are the nodes with their potential powers of development. This is the "Staff of Mercury" – the Caduceus.

Goethe described the upward growth as a gradual enhancement – the dense substances or heavier material below giving way, and transforming into lighter and finer ones. In this way, the plant grows at each stage, raising earthly-matter to become more and more receptive of the light. The plant is able through its upward striving, to lift itself from the more earthly connection and to make visible the forces that are working down onto the earth from cosmic space.

In his lectures on Agriculture, Rudolf Steiner spoke often about the relationships between the plants and the influences streaming into them from the periphery, from the cosmos. In one lecture he spoke as follows:

"Look at the green plant-leaves. The green leaves in their form and thickness, and in their greenness too, carry an earthly element, but they would not be green

4. R Steiner, Berlin, 1908.

unless the cosmic force of the sun were also living in them. And even more so when you come to the coloured flower. Therein are living not only the cosmic forces of the sun, but also the additional forces which the sun-forces receive from the distant planets – Mars, Jupiter and Saturn. In this way we must look at all plant growth. Then, when we observe the rose, in its red colour we shall see the forces of Mars. Or when we look at the yellow sunflower – and it is not quite rightly so named, it is named on account of its form; as to its yellowness it should really be called the Jupiter-flower. For the force of Jupiter supplementing the cosmic force of the sun, brings forth the white or yellow colour in the flowers. And when we approach the Chicory (*Cichorium Intybus*), we shall sense in the bluish colour the influence of Saturn, supplementing that of the sun. We can recognise Mars in the red flower, Jupiter in the yellow or white, Saturn in the blue, while in the green leaf we see essentially the sun itself. But that which shines out in the colouring of the flower also works as a force strongly in the root. For the forces and influences that live and abound in the distant planets are working down below in the earthly soil."[5]

The Sun and the Moon

In an early phase of earth evolution, when the rhythms of day and night began, physical forms rose up out of the earth's watery element. These were the forebears of the present plant kingdom. Early plant forms were influenced by the astral activity of the sun, and the ethereal nature of the earth.

In our present time, spiritual forces stream down to the earth within the rays of sunlight. This influences the process of expansion in plant growth. From the moon, the plant receives its contracting processes, where the plant is gathered together in the stem or at the base of a leaf. There is a continuous interplay of contraction and expansion within the plant's growing activity. In this, the rhythmic interplay of sunshine and moonshine is made visible. The sun expands the leaf and the flower; the moon contracts within the nodal points and in the seed formation.

The influences of the sun live strongly in the green leaf, in the whole process of the leaf's growth in an interplay between the flower and the root. In this way, the sun-quality can be considered to be related to the "diaphragm" of the earth – to all that weaves and breathes in this middle realm of the earth's surface.

The moon's influence intensifies the vitality of the earth, enhancing the growth process to the point of reproduction. With the rays of the moon, the whole cosmos is reflected back onto the earth. All the influences which stream in from the starry heavens are reflected and rayed down from the moon onto the earth, creating a powerfully organised cosmic force, assisting the seeding process of the plant, especially at the time of the full moon.

5. Rudolf Steiner, *Agriculture,* Lecture 2, given in Koberwitz, 10 June, 1924.
6. Reference and suggested reading: Rudolf Steiner, *Agriculture*, Ibid.

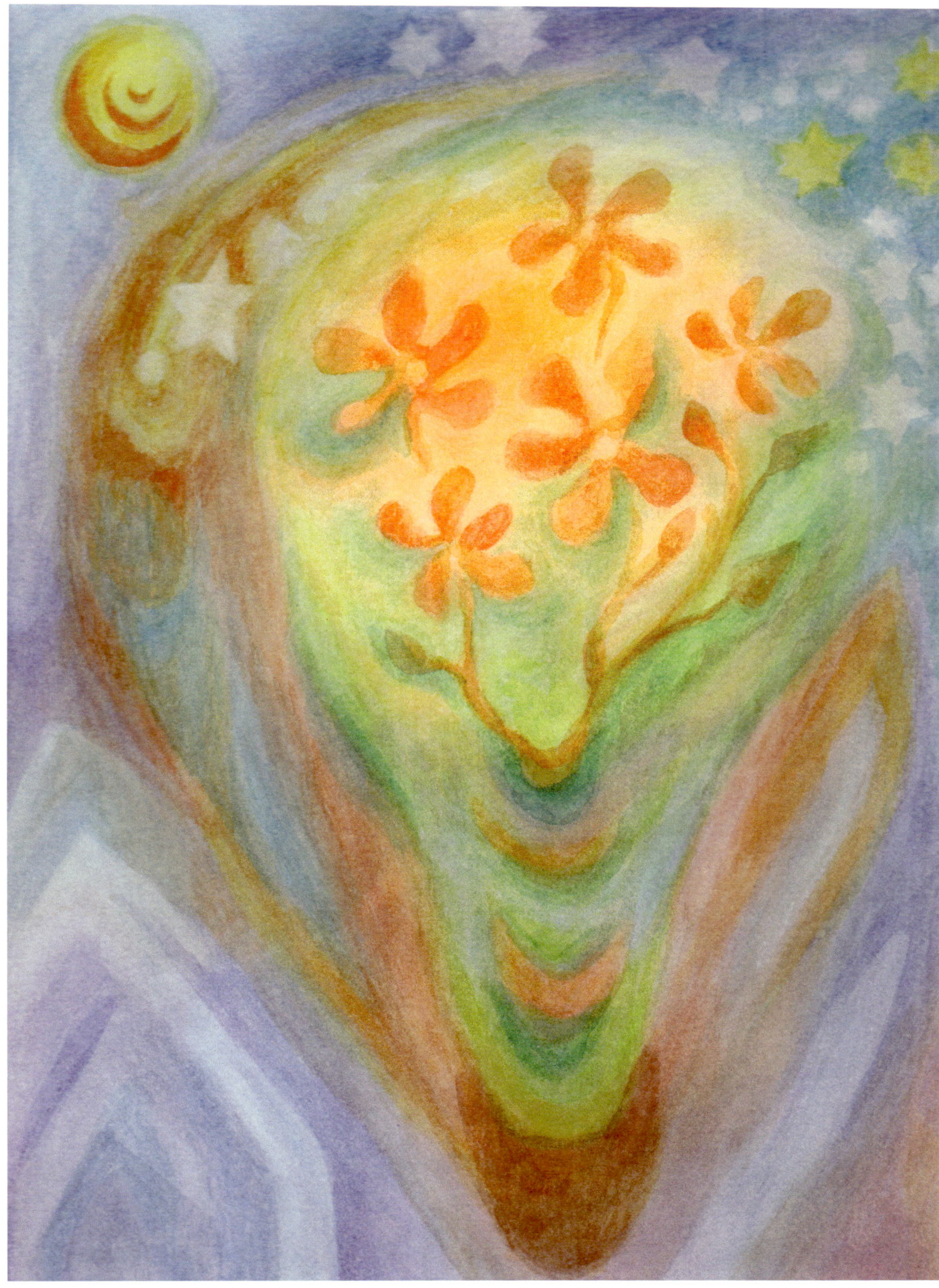

Fig. 24. *Influences of the Cosmos* (author)

Weeds and medicinal plants are particularly influenced by the moon and its phases. This knowledge was put into practice by many folk-cultures throughout the world, who planted, tended and harvested their crops according to the phases of the moon. Water also helps to distribute the lunar forces in the earthly realm; there is a definite connection between the moon, and the water on the earth (this can be observed for example in the tidal variations of rivers and seas, according to the Moon's phases). When rainy days are followed by a full moon, tremendous forces rise up and shoot into all the growth of the plants – here something colossal is taking place on earth.[6]

Whitsun

Rudolf Steiner spoke of the festival of Whitsuntide as being a festival of flowers. He spoke of gaining a true feeling for Whitsun through the opening of the buds and blossoms of the spring:

"We will perceive in the flower-decked earth the earthly image of what flows together in the picture of Christ's Ascension, and the descent of the tongues of fire upon the heads of the disciples which followed later. The heart of man as it opens may be symbolised by the flower opening itself to the sun; and what pours down from the sun, giving the flower the fertilising power it needs, may be symbolised by the tongues of fire descending upon the heads of the disciples."[7]

7. Rudolf Steiner, 'Whitsun: the Festival of the Free Individuality', Hamburg, Whitsunday, 1910 included in *The Festivals and their Meanings*.

CHAPTER TWO: THE PLANT IN ALCHEMY AND THE MYSTICAL ROSE

> "Red Rose, proud Rose, sad Rose of all my days!
> Come near me, while I sing the ancient ways ..."
> W. B. Yeats

From the third to the seventeenth centuries AD alchemists developed difficult experiments in esoteric training, working in secrecy, both for protection against the risk of persecution and out of a profound spiritual modesty. They also wished to "potentise" their work, veiling it from the "profanity" of the world. Their notebooks are full of marvellous and complicated drawings, ciphers, symbols and emblems, which, when carefully decoded can reveal their spiritual experiences and their knowledge of substances. Recurrent symbols were used to represent a four-fold image of the human being, namely:

The Ego — The higher self; the true human, the human proper.

Represented by: images of rex and regina (the king and queen); a hermaphrodite; homunculus. Also indicated by the chemical element of hydrogen; by the fire, and by symbols for the spirit.

The Astral Body — The human as a creature; a sentient being; the soul-feeling realm.

Represented by: images of animals, birds, reptiles. Also by the chemical element of carbon dioxide; by the element of air and by images of the soul.

The Etheric Body — The vitality of life; the true life-force; the vegetative plant realm.

Represented by: images of flowers, plants and of trees. Also by the element of oxygen; by the element of water; and by the atmosphere.

The Physical Body — The sensory sphere; the mineral realm; solid matter.

Represented by: images of metals, stones; by the chemical element of nitrogen, the element of earth. Also indicated by the senses and cognition.

The tree was the alchemists' supreme symbol of unity and of uniting. It appeared in countless variations, representing both the sense-perceptible and the super-sensible. The Tree image was used to represent the entire terrestrial atmosphere which for alchemists, included the sun, the moon and the planetary system. The Tree was a symbol for the holistic picture of the planetary organism in the full scope of its majestic, organic beauty.

Jan Baptiste van Helmont (1577-1644), who claimed to have achieved the Stone (i.e. alchemical illumination), is credited with the "discovery", or defining, of carbon dioxide, which he called "gas sylvestre" in reference to the Alchemical Tree. Oxygen was called "the first matter", and nitrogen "Azoth". Alchemists at this time must have experienced a conscious and vital interplay with the atmosphere around them. The atmospheric sheath of the planet was alive to them (as it was to the ancient Greeks), and their awareness of the Tree and its effluvium of living processes echoed the natural clairvoyance of earlier centuries. This special cognition served as a bridge between the earlier natural clairvoyance of the elements, which was fading away, and the new Christ-inspired etheric vision of the present and future.

The alchemists experienced this unity in their great work, as they investigated nature's interconnectedness.

Paracelsus (1493-1541) knew of the Christ Infusion, which he called the iliaster, or "star matter", a word made from ilius – matter, and astra – star. He described a mesh of Infusion-threads, or iliastri, throughout the atmosphere, as if the blood were developing into a vast, earth-ensheathing "tissue" of spiritual substance. Paracelsus points to the indwelling Christ as Spirit of the Earth and as a presence in the atmosphere in his writing: "In the whole Idea, there is but One Man, the same is extracted from the iliastrum and is the protoplast." Through their vision of the Tree and the streaming metals (senses, or substances), which poured in from the planets, the alchemists gained contact with the living, radiant spirit of the earth. For them, nature was a mystery-experience in which they were engaged as self-initiating agents. They aimed to take up nature's processes and to advance them by concentrating them in the crucible of human consciousness.

The alchemist Henry Khunrath (1560-1605) described the outpouring at Golgotha as an atmospheric diffusion of "costly Catholic[1] Rosy-coloured Blood and Aetheric Water that flows Azothically from the side of the innate Son of the Great World, when opened by the power of the Art". To the alchemists, Azoth (nitrogen) served as the physical medium for the Divine Blood through which they contacted the divine effluvia as a mystical sensation or spiritual experience, by the power of the Art.

1. Catholic = all embracing; universal.

<u>Rudolf Steiner – Verses and Poetry</u>

Rudolf Steiner wrote an enigmatic meditative verse which also contains an alchemical "substance". It embodies a mystical experience not dissimilar to that which Khunrath perceived.

The verse reads as follows:

"In light-and-air of Spirit Lands

There grow the roses of the Soul.

And their red radiates

Into the weight of the earth;

It is, in the Being of Man,

Fashioned into the form of the heart;

It shines in the forces of the blood

As rose red of the earth

Streaming forth once more

Into the spirit realms."

And in the original German:

"In der Lichtesluft des Geisteslandes

Da erblüh'n die Seelenrosen

Und ihr Rot erstrahlet

In die Erdenschwere;

Es wird im Menschenwesen

Zum Herzgebild verdichtet;

Es Strahlet in der Bluteskraft

Als das Erdenrosenrot

In die Geistesfelder wieder hin." [2]

This verse is quite mysterious. It requires an inner effort, an inner "work" to penetrate it and to sense its living imaginative reality.

2. Rudolf Steiner, published in *Verses and Meditations*.

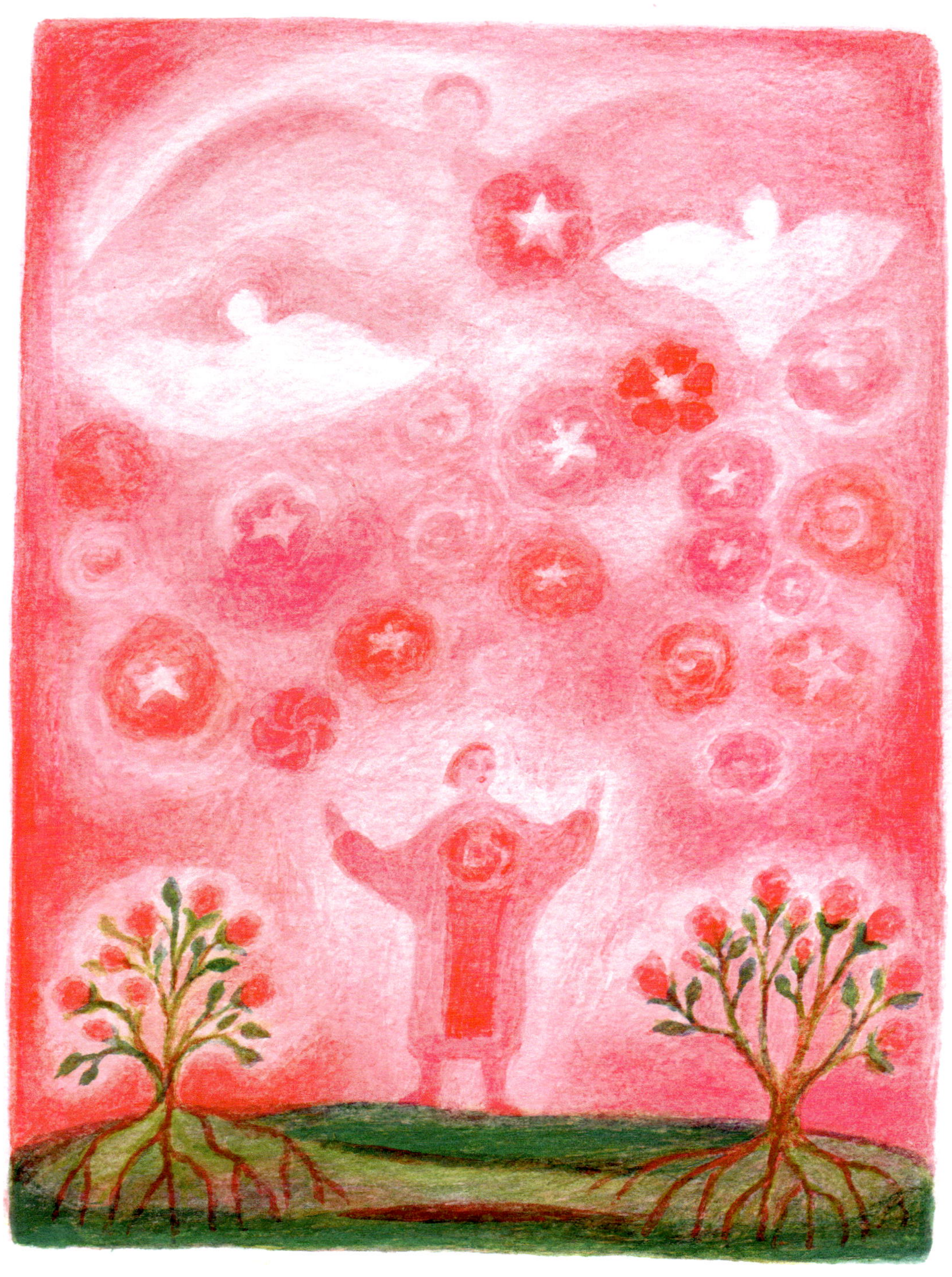

Fig. 25. *"In light-and-air of Spirit-Lands.*

There grow the roses of the Soul" (author)

An archetypal alchemical interplay between spirit, soul and the physical world is given in its mantric form, with reference in particular to the images of the rose. The spiritual activity of the soul-roses is creating a rose-like structure within the human heart. This is indeed a physical reality, as the unfolding petals of a rosebud are similar in their proportion and form to that of the muscular structure within the chambers of the heart.[3]

The rose has another mystical aspect in its connection with the human soul. I quote from an article written by H. Reid Shaw: "The Rose receives into her ethereal life the experiences of our earliest childhood. These memories, filled with wonder, impart to the Rose her incomparable beauty and delicate scent. Tender recollections of our childhood indwell the Rose and bestow upon her the capacity to renew our hope in earthly life and to refresh our appetites for all that comprises it. Thus does the Rose help us to perceive the redemptive value of the thorns upon our path as well as to cherish the sweetness of life's flowers".[4]

The mystical aspects of the rose have inspired many poets, who pay tribute in imaginative verses to its spiritual nature as well as to its earthly beauty. Here are just a few:

<u>Traditional Mexican Song</u>

"We can only sleep

only dream,

it is not true, no

it is not the truth

that we come

to live forever on this earth.

For the grass of spring

our hearts are destined,

they will grow green again,

will open their petals;

for we are as a rose-tree

that blossoms

then withers away."

Quoted in *El pueblo del Sol* in *Ancient Mexican Art.*

3. For further reading refer to Lawrence Edwards' *The Vortex of Life.*
4. H. Reid Shaw, 'Flower Essence Therapy and Rosicrucianism' in *New View*, Summer 2006.

<u>'The Mystery'</u>

"He came and took me by the hand

Up to a red rose tree,

He kept His meaning to Himself

But gave a rose to me.

I did not pray Him to lay bare

The mystery to me

Enough the rose was Heaven to smell

And His own face to see."

Ralph Hodgson
Published in *Come Hither* collected by W. de la Mare.

<u>Song</u>

What is there hid in the heart of a rose,

Mother-mine?

Ah, who knows, who knows, who knows?

A Man that died on a lonely hill

May tell you, perhaps, but none other will,

 Little child.

What does it take to make a rose,

Mother-mine?

The God that died to make it knows

It takes the world's eternal wars

It takes the moon and all the stars

It takes the might of heaven and hell

And the everlasting Love as well

 Little child.

Alfred Noyes
Published in *Come Hither* collected by Walter de la Mare.

And to conclude ...

"Thanks to the human heart by which we live,
Thanks to its joys, its hopes, its fears,
The meanest flower that blows can give
Thoughts that do often lie too deep for tears."
William Wordsworth

PART FOUR

CHAPTER ONE: GOETHE'S ARCHETYPAL PLANT

"In selfless contemplation of Nature, we can so train our imaginative faculties
that they become an instrument of cognition."
Rudolf Steiner

J. W. von Goethe (1749-1832) developed an approach to observing nature based upon an awakened, conscious faculty of observation. As he observed and contemplated nature, Goethe was able to train his imaginative abilities in such a way that they became conscious faculties of cognition. He perceived the truthfulness of the phenomena itself. When observing a plant, for example, his idea of the archetype became apparent within the phenomena of the plant itself. The phenomena of the actual plant was similar to the ideal reality which lay behind it, and which brought it into physical manifestation. He realised that the idea of an archetypal plant exists behind, or within, all individual plants and plant species. He knew that insight should come with a healthy, unbiased sight. Combined what he could see physically with an inner spiritual activity of seeing, he allowed his unbiased thinking to interpret the language of the phenomena. What his thinking perception revealed was stimulated by the phenomena of the plant itself – it was as though he could see with newly awakened eyes. His own thoughts met with, and united with, the archetypal thought which had created the plant.

In this manner, Goethe's awakened faculties were expressed in his whole scientific outlook. In selfless contemplation of nature, he could so train his imagination that it became for him an instrument of cognition. Thus was born the Goetheanistic scientific approach – a method of unprejudiced direct observation which can be applied to various fields of scientific inquiry.

<u>The Goethean Method</u>

Goethe's artistic nature wanted to enlighten the being of things, to illuminate the prototypes behind the visible world. When he observed nature it brought ideas to meet him; he felt intimately connected with nature. He experienced the continuous streaming of world events flowing through his consciousness, and so felt that the world of ideas was nothing other than the creative, active power of nature. He did not stand outside of things, to think about them objectively, but entered into them, drawing forth what lived and worked within them. To Goethe, the creative act of an artist producing a work of art was no different to the way in which nature created its works. When travelling in Italy, he wrote:

"The great works of art have been brought forth by human beings according to true and natural laws, as have the greatest works of Nature."[1]

Philosophic activity was also related to artistic creativity. The philosopher created profound thoughts to clarify perceptions; the artist created works of art. To Goethe, art and nature comprised one unified realm of truth. The capacity for artistic activity was, as he saw it, similar to the capacity for knowing nature. Both merged into and overlapped each other. Concerning the style of the artist, he acknowledged that it rested upon the deepest foundations of knowledge regarding the being, or essence, of things. The artist realised the ideas of nature and was able to show how nature *could* look, when these ideas or archetypes were brought into the sense-perceptible world in a work of art.

When Goethe's intuitive spirit turned to nature, perception and idea joined themselves together in a unity. Hence, the reciprocal working of idea and perception was a spiritual breathing: through being able to observe inwardly how ideas lived within consciousness, inner life had objective validity. Outer viewing of the world was filled with living spiritualised perceptions so that he was no longer a stranger to nature, but felt united with it. Both reason and imagination needed to be active, and to penetrate into the inner aspect of phenomena in order to grasp elements of existence. He knew that, "nature is a development from a living mysterious whole, to the manifold particular phenomena which fill space and time. The mysterious whole is the world of the idea ... When a person really succeeds in raising himself to the idea, and taking his start from the idea, and succeeds in grasping the particulars of perception, he then accomplishes the same thing that nature does when it lets its creations go forth out of the mysterious whole."[2]

Human faculties of imagination mirror that great imagination which is creating all of nature, and its manifold shapes, forms and colours. The world being can reveal itself to human imagination, because it also lives within the human being. The inner reality of being is without, it is all around us; the outer being of nature also lies within us.

Goethe sketched a symbolic plant for Schiller, after they had both attended a meeting of the Society for Natural Research in Jena (near Weimar). His drawing was intended to express the being that lives in every individual plant, no matter which particular forms the plant might assume. On 17 April 1787, Goethe, in Palermo, wrote: "There must, after all, be such a one! How would I otherwise know that this or that formation is a plant, if they were not all formed according to the same model." For him, like the actual and individual plant, the symbolic or archetypal plant was an objective reality.

1. Quoted in *Goethe's World View* by R Steiner.
2. Rudolf Steiner, *Goethe's World View.*

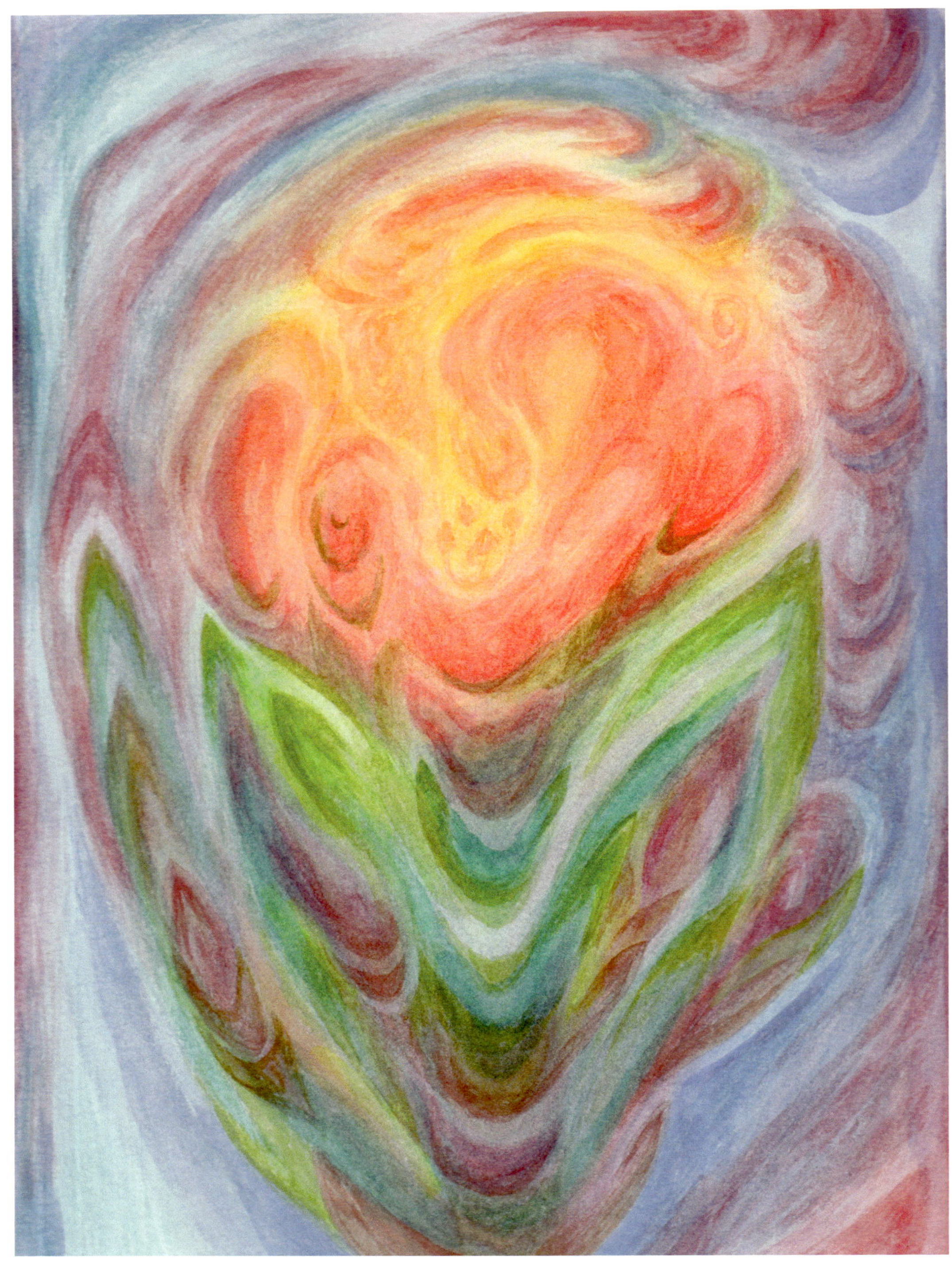

Fig. 26. *Archetypal Plant 1* (author)

CHAPTER TWO: THE METAMORPHOSIS OF PLANTS

In his famous poem on plant metamorphosis, J. W. von Goethe embodied in poetic, imaginative form the intimacy of his plant observations. He writes of the cycle of plant growth in all its stages, activities and manifestations.

<u>Plant Metamorphosis</u> by J. W. von Goethe

You wonder, Beloved,

at the thousandfold

mingled multitude of flowers

in the garden.

You listen to their many names

which, one after the other,

are always resounding in your ears.

All their forms bear a resemblance

yet none is quite like another;

And so their choir suggests

a mysterious law, when

you contemplate now

how slowly but surely the Plant-form

stage-by-stage guided

develops to blossom and fruit.

From out of the seed it develops

just as soon as the earth's

silently fertile womb

lovingly gives it to life.

And to the allurement of light

the Holy, eternally weaving,
delicate forms of sprouting leaves
bestow themselves now to its care.
The unified, fundamental force
slept in the seed;
the primal archetype lay
self-enclosed, curled under
the leaf, root and shoot,
only half-formed and colourless.
Thus the kernel preserves
and protects in dryness

an un-stirring life,
which swells from surrounding darkness
striving eagerly upwards, when
to gentle moisture entrusted.

But the gesture stays simple
in its first appearance.
Thereupon, a following shoot
arises, renewing
node upon node towering,
ever the first form again.

But not always identical
for it diversely engenders
fully developed, you see,
always the following leaf,
more out-stretched and more jagged,

more divided in points and parts.

But here Nature holds
with her almighty hands
the formative process.

And softly she leads
to fulfilment of form.
And soon the shape shows
a more tender appearance.
The accelerating growth
of the striving extremities
quietly holds itself back,
and the ribs of the stalk
expand themselves fully out.
A marvellous formation delights the beholder.
Circularly placing themselves now
proportioned and without number,
the smaller leaves placed
near the ones bearing their likeness.
Around the Axis crowded,
the heaped calyx splits open
freeing the supreme form –
the coloured corona itself.
This glory heralds a new creation.
The colourful petals
sense the heavenly Hand,
and quickly contracts together
the most delicate form,

two-fold they stream out

pre-destined for uniting.

Intimately now they stand

the gracious pairs, all together.

Manifold they arrange themselves

around the living Altar.

The nuptial god approaches,

hovering; and splendid

sweet perfume

fills the surrounding air.

Now sporadically swell

simultaneously, uncountable seeds,

sheltered in the womb of swelling fruit.

And here Nature closes

her wheel of eternal activity

yet a new cycle directly

follows the last year's on.

Thus is the chain

prolonged from age to age,

so that, like each of its parts,

the whole may become a living creation.

Author's translation

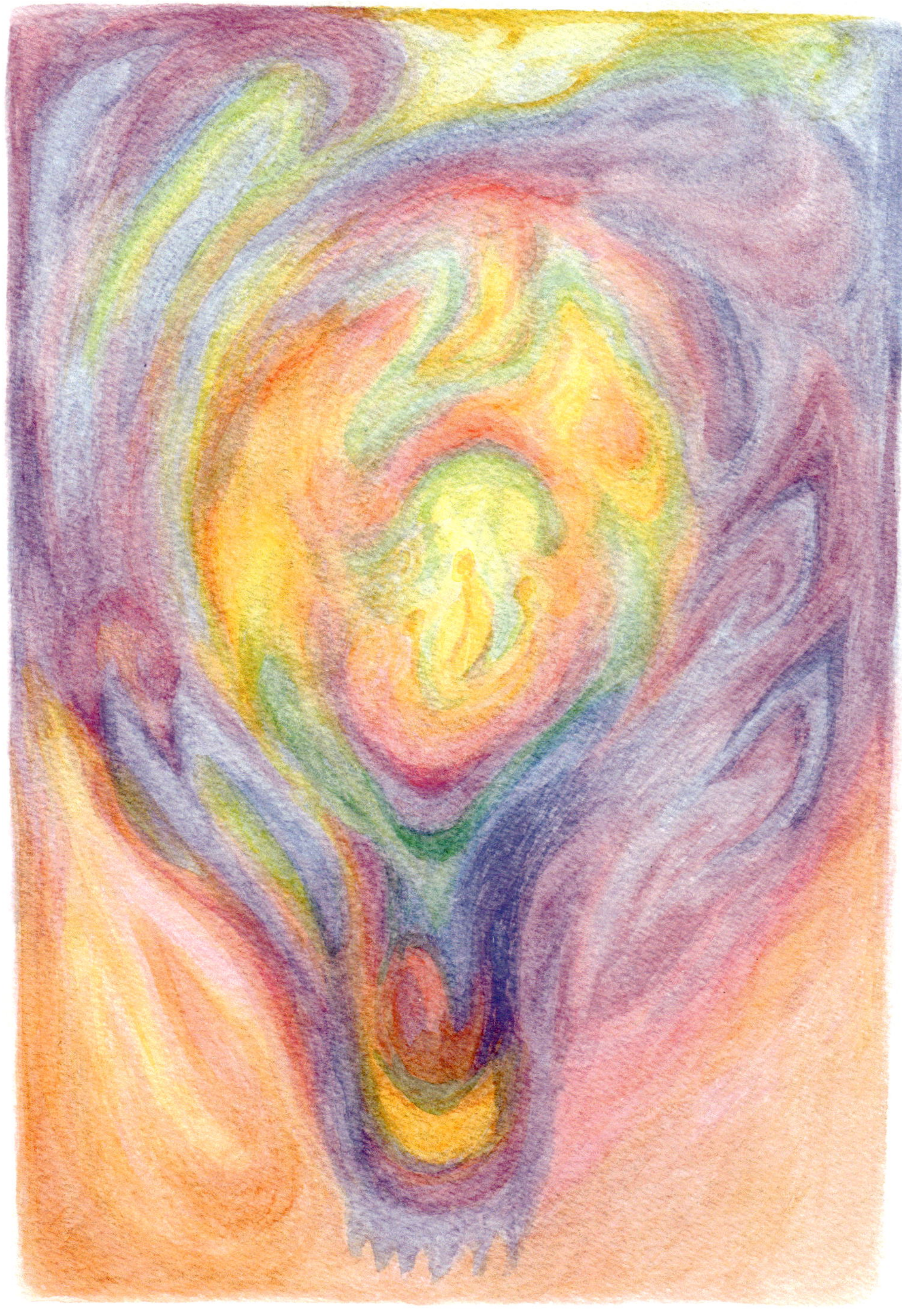

Fig. 27. *Archetypal Plant 2* (author)

CHAPTER THREE: THE SOUL CALENDAR VERSES

Rudolf Steiner wrote fifty-two meditative verses, one for each week of the year. They relate to cosmic and world events throughout the changing course of the seasons and festivals, and to the inner experiences which the human soul reflects accordingly.

Each verse can be used as a meditation for its appropriate week, giving an imaginative insight to the soul's responses to the cosmic world-all, and to nature. In working with the soul-calendar verses, one's own consciousness is enhanced and enriched.

The Soul Calendar Verse which corresponds to the week of May 12 – 18 reads as follows:

There has arisen from its narrow limits

My self, and finds itself

As revelation of all worlds

Within the sway of time and space;

The world as archetype divine,

Displays to me at every turn

The truth of my own likeness.

The German reads:

Es ist erstanden aus der Eigenheit

Mein Selbst und findet sich

Als Weltenoffenbarung

In Zeit- und Raumeskräften;

Die Welt, sie zeigt mir überall

Als göttlich Urbild

Des eignen Abbilds Wahrheit.

This verse reflects the soul experiences which J. W. Goethe had, in his intense relationship with nature and the world. His perceptions rose from their narrow limitations to see that his own higher self was reflected within the world, within time and space. The world around him became a divine archetype revealing the truth of his own being.

This particular verse bears a wonderful relationship to the *Archetypal Plant* painting, which was painted during the corresponding week (May 12 -18) in 1924.

"... in the tiniest plant we are made aware of the nature of light from beyond the earth. Through an ascent in contemplation, we can perceive the diffference between the earthly and physical which holds sway in the life-less world, and the non-earthly ethereal which abounds in all living things."

Rudolf Steiner, from *Anthroposophical Leading Thoughts*

"Let us consider the rhythmic processes in the plant and the human being. The plant has no such rhythm as our breathing, and it saps do not pulsate in any kind of cardiac rhythm. Both its exchange of substances and its growth unfold in harmony with the living rhythms of the earth, with alternations of summer and winter, day and night, rain and sunshine. The rhythmic processes which have in us become internalised and individualised are for the plant, embedded in the external, outer-world ... their breath is the wind, their blood the water, their heart the life-endowing sun."

Paraphrased from *The Plant* by Gerbert Grohmann

PART FIVE

CHAPTER ONE: PLANTS AND THE ELEMENTAL BEINGS

The plant kingdom has a number of invisible "helping hands". These are the elemental beings: gnomes, undines, sylphs and salamanders. Different traditions, folklore and legends from various countries all seem to include references to the fairies, or the wee-folk.

Although in our present times we can no longer (on the whole) see these invisible helpers, they are nevertheless present in our surroundings. There have been a number of recent books written and published concerning the elemental beings, by people who are able to have direct contact with them. In some cases, the elemental beings themselves will choose to whom they wish to make their presence and their work discernible. The information and descriptions in this chapter have been sourced from lectures given by Rudolf Steiner, whose clairvoyance revealed much about their characteristics and their activities.

<u>Gnomes</u>

Gnomes inside the earth bear the ideas of the universe. They do not like the earth itself, so they fill themselves entirely with ideas of the universe. Their consciousness is entirely understanding, and filled with direct perception.

F. Martin Duncan wrote in *The Life of the Plants*, "The plant drinks with its roots, which also fix the plant firmly in the soil. This they do so thoroughly and cleverly that they might well imagine that roots have minds to think about and understand what they have to do."

Gnomes receive their thoughts from the plants, and laugh at human foolishness. It is from their antipathy towards the earth that gnomes gain the power of pushing the plants up out of the earth. With the fundamental force of their being, they increasingly thrust away the earthly and it is this thrusting that determines the upward direction of the plants' growth - they push the plants up with them.

<u>Undines</u>

Once the plant has passed up out of the moist-earthly element and into the sphere of the moist-airy, the plant develops leaves. Here we have the water spirits, the undines, at work. They give themselves over to the weaving and working of the whole cosmos in the moist-airy element. They dream, living in the etheric element of water. They weave their way around the leaves, dreaming the uniting and dispersing of substances – they are the world-chemists.

Sylphs

In the airy element, there are the sylphs. They are sensitive to air movements within the atmosphere. Bird-flights give the sylphs a feeling of ego or self-hood. Sylphs become the bearer of cosmic love through the atmosphere. They convey light to the plant, and actually weave the invisible form of the archetypal plant within the plant from light, and from the chemical working of the undines. They carry the action of the light ether into the plant's blossoms.

Salamanders

After the plant has grown through the sphere of the sylphs, the plant comes into the sphere of the elemental fire-spirits. These elemental beings live in the warmth-light realm. They gather up warmth and carry it into the blossoms, the pollen providing little "air-ships" to enable the fire-spirits to carry warmth into the seed. The fire-light beings are known as salamanders, and they accompany the bees and butterflies, which are surrounded by an aura. This aura is actually a salamander.

Each elemental being carries a certain power, or force, for the world. Salamanders are sacrificial; sylphs carry love, undines weave within magnetism, and gnomes work within gravity. The plant is an outer expression of the inter-working of world-love and world-sacrifice, with world-gravity and world-magnetism, as organised and developed by the elemental beings. Without this working and inter-weaving of the gnomes, undines, sylphs and salamanders, we would have no crops, plants or trees. Their invisible presence sustains life for us.

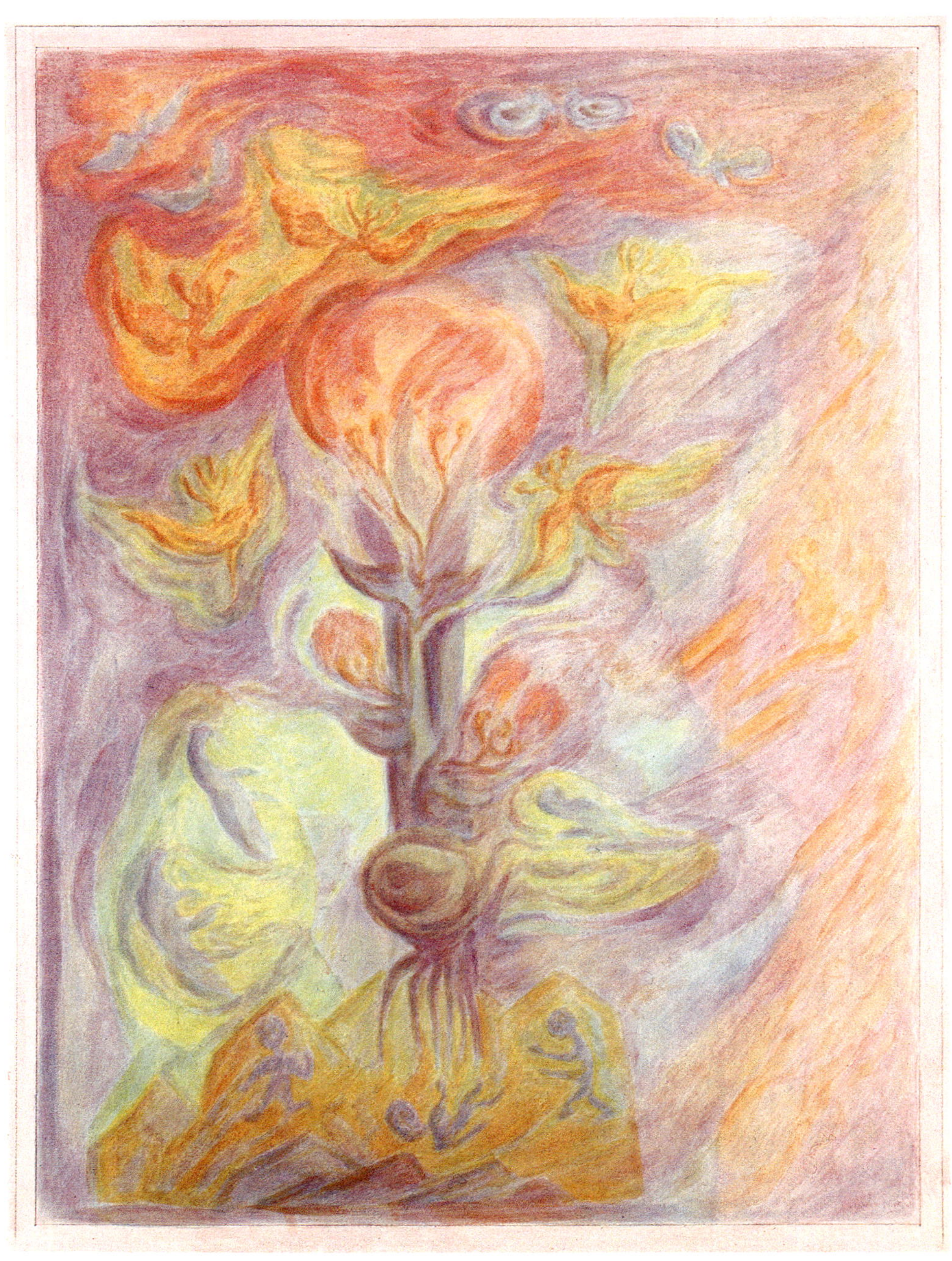

Fig. 28. *Plant with elemental beings,* Gerard Wagner

CHAPTER TWO:
AN ALCHEMY OF COLOUR:
THE COLOURS AS THEY REPRESENT THE ETHERS

"Fire, Air, Water, Earth were but the visible garb, the symbols of the informing, invisible
Souls or Spirits – the Cosmic gods to whom worship was offered by the simple , and
respectful recognition by the wiser."
The Secret Doctrine, H. P. Blavatsky ('On the Elements')

The four elements: earth, fire, air and water, have relationships to the signs of
the zodiac. Through these particular relationships to the starry worlds they can
be placed into connections with the four ethers, which work into earthly and
cosmic processes.

The zodiacal earth signs, Taurus, Virgo and Capricorn, are assigned the life-ether,
which has the colour violet.

The zodiacal water signs, Cancer, Scorpio and Pisces, are assigned the chemical-
ether, which has the colour blue.

The zodiacal air signs, Gemini, Libra and Aquarius, are assigned the light-ether,
which has the colour yellow.

The zodiacal fire signs, Aries, Leo and Sagittarius, are assigned the warmth-ether,
which has the colour red.

The four ethers work into the four elements as etheric formative forces. They
are not physical; they stream down to the earth from the periphery, from the
heavens. Light- ether, for example, is everywhere – it works within the light
but it is a finer substance, finer even than light. When it is active in an organism
light-ether brings about an expansion and an extension into space, bringing about
the activity of growth. Just as light rays out, or shines out from a source, so
does a living organism begin at a point or a particular "beginning", which can be a
seed, a nodule, an ovum or a growth-tip – and rays out, or extends and expands
into space from there. Although light-ether originates in the outer peripheral
surroundings of earth, its activity is to draw or to expand organic matter
towards that periphery. Sunlight draws the plant upwards, and the upper part of
the plant is lifted away from the earth, overcoming gravity. The organic action
of the light-ether is to bring about expansion. In the archetypal plant painting,
yellow surrounds the flower at the top. It brings an activity of light, opening
and lifting the flower, and to the bud also, on the right-hand side. On the left,
the yellow penetrates into the darker violet which opens into two and seems
to reach upwards into the yellow above; the pink-violetish colour appears to be

penetrated, to be "opened" by the yellow.

Chemical-ether has three different aspects, which Rudolf Steiner defined. He gave three different names — tone-ether, chemical-ether, and number-ether — depending on which sphere of activity, and in which substances this ether was working in. It is an ether which originates in the cosmic periphery. The activity, or force of levity is one of its characteristics, which can be seen in the upward-striving growth of plants as they overcome the forces of gravity. It also harmonises and brings about the ordering of different parts of a whole, so that they are brought into relationship with each other. In chemical processes it is active in the dissolving and distributing of substances. In plant-life it is found everywhere as number-ether, dividing the leaf nodes, and ordering them in harmonious rhythmical patterns as they spiral up plant stems.

In the *Archetypal Plant* painting, the chemical-ether is shown in its manifest activities in the deep-blue colouring of the watery sac at the lower part of the plant, and extending up the right-hand side. This shows the surrounding, harmonising activity of the chemical- ether within watery substances. The stem of the plant and its shooting buds are also a deep blue. This blue indicates the growth dynamic which is overcoming gravity in the stem — also the chemical-ether — and the arrangement of the leaf-shoots which shows the placement-activity of the number-ether, as it arranges the buds in their numerically and spatially proportioned relationships along the stem.

The life-ether is found in the realm of living things, and arises together with the earth element. Life-ether gives the organism its own form, and as its name suggests, it creates living entities, beings (plants, animals, humans), which are alive. It holds its shape, giving form and spatial orientation. It enables a living being to create a boundary (a skin, a membrane) and brings about the healing processes when injury occurs, seeking always to create a living whole, to regenerate and to heal so that an organism is restored to its completeness. In the *Archetypal Plant* painting, the life-ether is painted in a violet-magenta colour. Careful observation shows that there is violet-magenta in different places throughout the whole painting. The roots stretching down into the blue enveloping sac below the large brown corm or bulb, are violet-magenta; it overlaps and surrounds the brown bulb and the blue stem, and there is also violet-magenta in the red flower. Life-ether permeates the whole plant, forming, vitalising, renewing and shaping.

The warmth-ether can be regarded as the primordial "mother substance" of existence, and is active within physical warmth, soul warmth and ripening processes. Where warmth is found, in space and within living beings, there is movement. From the beginning of creation warmth existed; within warmth

exists the possibility of material being, and of the time processes of living,
growing and maturing. A person with warmth of soul is usually socially active,
sympathetic in their character and positive in outlook. The organic world
reaches its flowering, fruiting and seeding activities through the influence of
the warmth-ether. This cycle of maturation is permeated by the activity of
the warmth-ether, which also brings about the disappearance, the dying of the
physical plant, and the future potential which lies in the seed. In the *Archetypal
Plant* painting, the warmth-ether is shown in the colour red, which is mainly in
the flower. The smaller details of the stamens and pistils are also red, a slightly
warmer red than the surrounding petals. Although the *Archetypal Plant* is painted
onto a background which has been toned with blue, a delicate pinkish-red
surrounds the image, giving the mood of the warmth-ether, the warmth out of
which the whole plant could emerge.

Reference: *The Individuality of Colour,* E. Koch/G. Wagner.
See Chapters, 'The Aether-Colour-Bow' and 'A New Colour Circle'.

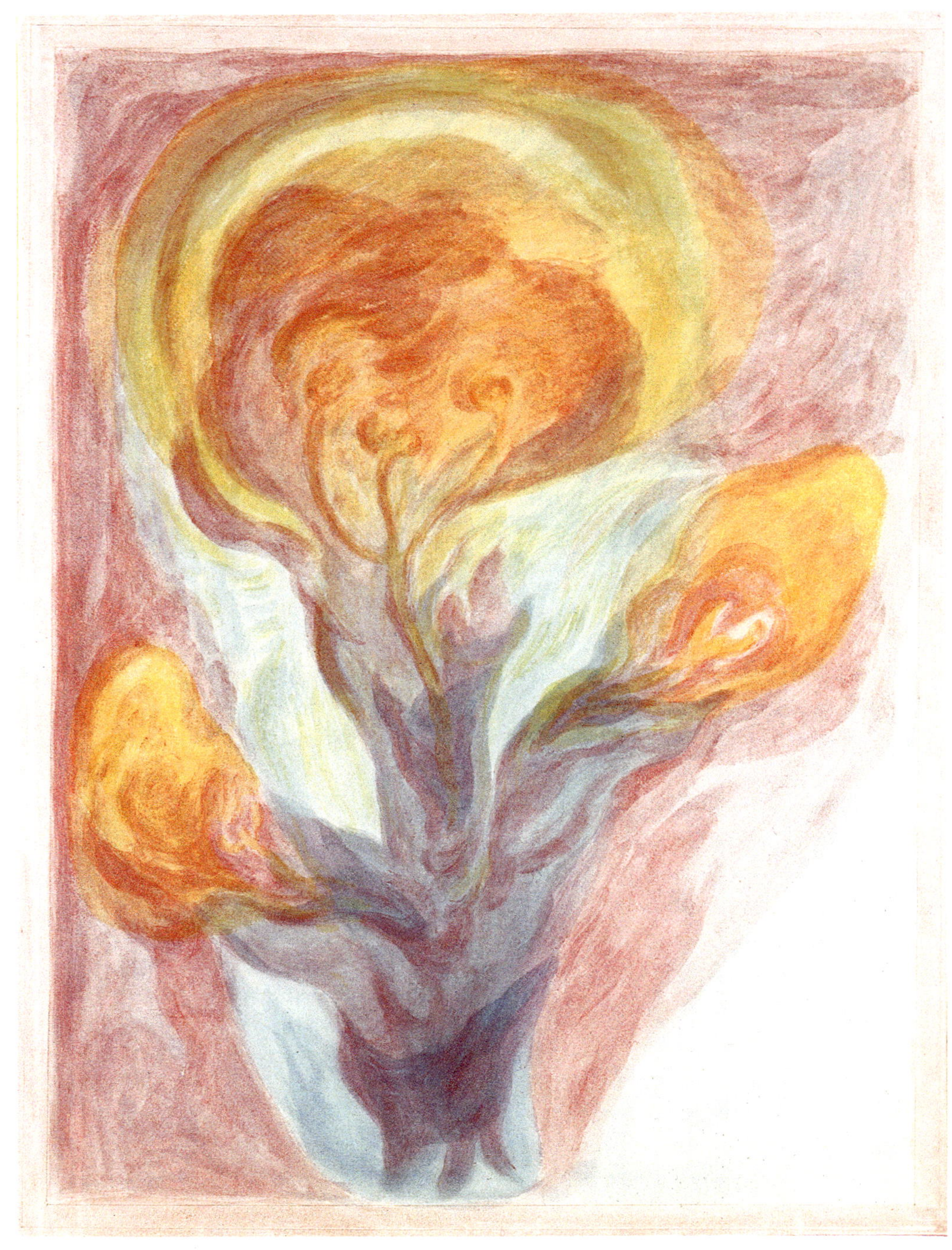

Fig. 29. *The Archetypal Plant*, Gerard Wagner

CHAPTER THREE:
THE COLOURS AS THEY REPRESENT THE ELEMENTS

"The plant is eating with its leaves. Each leaf is really a mouth, and all day long ... the plants
in the garden are sucking in food with their leaves. Of course we cannot see this, becasue
the plants are eating invisible food, a gas formed of carbon and oxygen, and it is this
carbonic acid that the plants are always so eagerly swallowing."
The Life of the Plants F. Martin Duncan

As well as considering the four ethers, we can also look at the elements which are the building blocks of all substances, and the ways in which they are visible in this painting. These elements are: carbon, sulphur, oxygen, nitrogen and hydrogen.

Steiner speaks of these elements from both physical and spiritual points of view. Concerning carbon, he said "... In effect, carbon is the bearer of all the creatively formative processes in Nature – it forms and shapes whatever is in Nature ... carbon is everywhere the great plastician (sculptor). It does not carry only itself in its black substantiality. Wherever we find it in full action and inner mobility, it bears within it the creative and formative cosmic pictures – the sublime cosmic Imaginations, out of which all that is formed in Nature must ultimately proceed."[1]

In the *Archetypal Plant* painting the colours which have a little black within them, that is, brown and indigo, form the large bulb and the stem. The stem and its many shoots are dark-blue (blue with a little black added), which provides the structural form of the plant. Inside the blue stem are two irregular 'columns' of a brownish colour.

The element of carbon is not visible as black, but black has been added to the blue of the stem to create indigo; and to the reddish-brown of the bulb and to the brownish gestures inside the stem. The black of carbon is concealed within the structural aspects of the plant. Rudolf Steiner described this as follows: "... whatever is formed and shaped in Nature ... carbon is everywhere the great sculptor ... carbon bears within it the sublime cosmic Imaginations, out of which all that is formed in Nature must ultimately proceed."

"Underlying all living things is a carbon-like scaffolding or framework – rigid or fluctuating as the case may be ... and along the paths of this framework, the spiritual moves through the world, working with the help of sulphur (in very fine dilution) ... In turn, this living carbon framework is permeated by the ethereal. Moistened with sulphur, the physical carrier of the ethereal is oxygen. The element of oxygen, with the help of sulphur, carries the life influences out of the universal ether into the

1. Rudolf Steiner, *The Agriculture Course.*

physical ... the ethereal moves, with the help of sulphur, along the paths of oxygen. The ethereal oxygen principle must find its way, to access the spiritual carbon-principle. The mediator of this process is nitrogen. Nitrogen guides the life into the form or configuration which is embodied in the carbon. Nitrogen carries the oxygen, so that it may fetch the carbon and get rid of it. Nitrogen, with the help of sulphur, builds the bridge between carbon and oxygen. And the spirituality which is working thus in nitrogen, is the astral spirituality in the earth's environment. Wherever nitrogen is, there the astral extends ... Nitrogen becomes the bearer of that mysterious sensitiveness which is poured out over the whole life of the earth ... Nitrogen is conscious of that which comes from the stars, and works itself out in the life of plants, in the life of Earth ... But all that is developed in the living plant or creature, structurally as in a fine and delicate design, must eventually be able to vanish again, into the cosmos. This is achieved by hydrogen, which carries all that is formed, alive and astral, out into the universe. In hydrogen the physical flows outward, carried by the sulphur, out into the void, into the realms of the cosmos into the universal all. Whenever carbon, hydrogen, nitrogen occur – in leaf or flower, calyx or root – everywhere they are bound to other substances in one form or another (in particular, to silica and calcium, or limestone)."[2]

In the *Archetypal Plant* the blue background can be seen to hydrogen and oxygen. In this painting, blue becomes the cosmic, universal all, that which creates the "back-drop" for the plant image. As a colour, blue is cool, and receding. It creates an impression of distance. Blue, representing the alchemical activities of oxygen and hydrogen, creates an ethereal space which is cool, far away and refreshing. Hydrogen, in particular, allows the physical to flow outwards into the cosmic universal all. We can gain an impression of this mood by gazing into a blue sky.

Surrounding the flower is a dull yellow, which could be termed a sulphurous yellow. Recalling the task of sulphur ("... in hydrogen, the physical flows outward, carried by the sulphur, out into the void, into the realms of the cosmos ..."), this dull yellow can be seen to be related to sulphur. The yellow surrounds the upper flowering part of the plant, as though it is a bridge between the crimson flower, and the blue background. We can form an analogy here, with this relationship between yellow and blue, and the relationship which sulphur and oxygen have: "... the element of oxygen, with the help of sulphur, carries the life influences out of the universal ether into the physical ... the ethereal moves with the help of sulphur, along the paths of oxygen."

When a plant flowers, astral forces stream into the plant from the cosmos to create the many beautiful colours. Here, in the *Archetypal Plant* the crimson flowers with their vermilion stamens, can be related to the activity of nitrogen, which is "conscious of that which comes from the stars ... it is the astral spirituality in the

2. Ibid.

earth's environment". Crimson also penetrates into the stem and leaves. When the crimson 'moves' from the roots through the stem and into the flower, we can sense how nitrogen builds a bridge between carbon and oxygen, as a mediator.

Finally, the rose-pink colour surrounding the whole motif can be seen imaginatively as representing hydrogen. This delicate colour surrounds and carries the plant image, extending out to the periphery of the painting.   "Hydrogen carries all that is formed, alive and astral, out into the universe. In hydrogen the physical flows outward, carried by the sulphur … out into the .. realms of the cosmos."

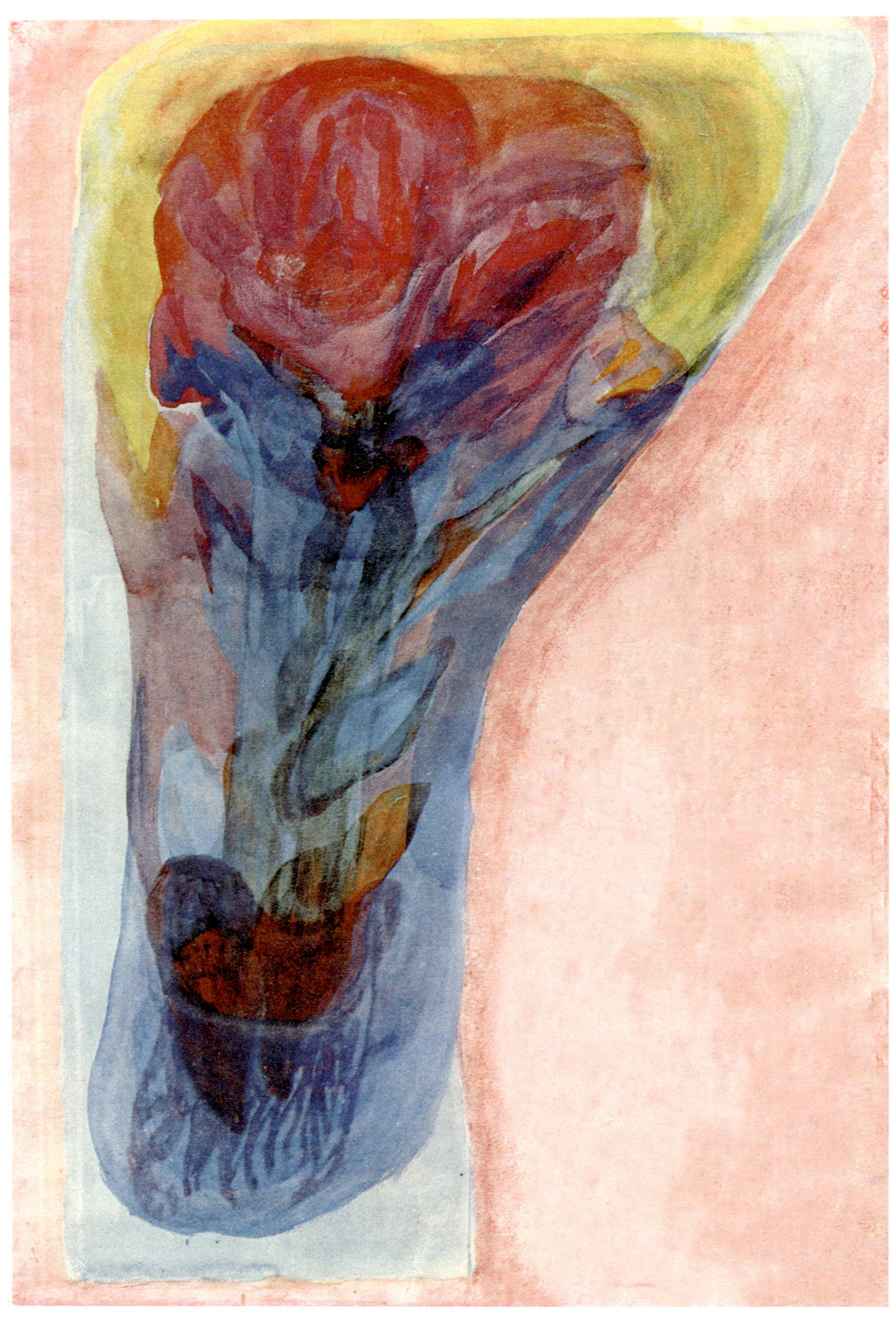

Fig. 30. Rudolf Steiner's *Archetypal Plant*

PART SIX

CHAPTER ONE: THE ARCHETYPAL PLANT PAINTING

Rudolf Steiner's water colour painting of the *Archetypal Plant* conveys the impression that the plant seems to be growing almost under water, or within a watery environment. The whole plant is surrounded by pale-blue, and is painted on a pale-blue background. (Careful observation of the image reveals that there is a layer of pale-blue beneath the colours.) This pale-blue wash (or toned background) creates a cool watery mood and influences the colours of the motif in their colour-tone, in their gesture, and in their form.

Unusually, in the painting, all of the plant structures including the bulb and roots which are normally concealed below the earth, have been depicted. The plant is shown in its entirety, in a representation similar to that used by botanical illustrators.

The large brownish bulb with its delicate descending violet roots, seems to be encased in a watery sac. The stem and shoots are coloured in a deeper blue, which is cool and transparent. The transparency of this blue is enhanced by a violet-magenta colour surrounding the area, which creates a slightly opaque surface on each side of the stem.

Inside the blue stem are two brownish gestures, extending from the lowest part of the flower (which actually penetrates into the upper stem), down to the bulb. They provide an inner structure and support, yet at the same time have a flowing, irregular form.

The crimson flowers bursting out of the thick blue stem are cup-shaped, forming broad chalice-like structures. They have bright vermilion-red pistils and stamens in their centres.

Above the flower, the surrounding yellow has a slightly dull appearance owing to the blue-toned background beneath the yellow. However, it nevertheless imparts a sun-like quality of warmth and light.

Small details here and there in orange, bring warmth and liveliness, giving a complimentary colour contrast to the blue.

The *Archetypal Plant* does not have a naturalistic quality; it cannot be found as a botanical species or as a plant growing in the garden. It seems to hover as though it exists in another world, which, in fact, it does. It exists as an archetype representing the processes in every plant and it belongs within the universal world-spirit which holds the idea or image of all plant forms.

It is interesting to note that Rudolf Steiner's painting has no green colouring in it. Above all other colours, green usually represents nature, life and growth; the whole of the plant world in its many aspects, is usually associated with the colour green because of the greenness of nature. It becomes apparent, then, that this painting is not one of a physical plant but an image depicting the colour activity of invisible formative forces as they create the spiritual template of the plant.

CHAPTER TWO: LUSTRE AND IMAGE COLOURS

" ... When we experience the life of colour we reach beyond ourselves and take part in
cosmic life. Colour is the soul element of nature and of the whole cosmos, and we have a
share in this soul element when we experience colour."
Rudolf Steiner[1]

In the lectures which he gave in May 1921[2], Rudolf Steiner made an interesting
distinction between what he termed lustre and image colours. The lustre, or
shining lustrous colours are yellow, blue and red. They have an inherent radiance,
and seem to shine out, each in their individual way, with a luminous quality.

The image colours, green, peach-blossom, black and white do not seem to shine or
radiate, but have a quality which is quieter, more at rest. These image colours have
an appearance which conveys something else. When we look at plants growing
in the garden, we can see the changes in the processes of growth, from the seed
to the sprouting, leafing, flowering, the forming of new seeds and the dying away.
These processes could not take place if the plant were a physical structure only,
for then the plant would belong to the mineral realm. The green plant owes its
existence and its growth processes to the etheric realm which is the source of
its life. But the plant's etheric body is not green. What is making the plant green
is its physical body which is the outcome, the result of etheric life processes. In
this way we experience the green as an image or picture, a representation of life-
forces, not the actual life-forces themselves. Green represents the lifeless image
of the living.

We can understand the colours black, peach-blossom (a bright pinkish magenta)
and also white as also being colours which represent something. Black is the
representative of something which is lacking life; it is an image of the lifeless.
Peach-blossom is found within the human soul (we can see this when someone
blushes for example). It can be experienced as a colour which is alive and can be
understood as the living image of the soul. Peach-blossom is not the soul itself,
but we see this colour when the soul reveals itself in certain circumstances. White
represents our experience of the spirit. We can understand white to be the soul's
image, or picture of the spirit.

In the *Archetypal Plant* painting we see mainly lustre colours: yellow, blue and red.
These colours which have their own radiance and shining lustrous qualities convey
the life of the plant in a directly perceptible way. Yellow is the shining radiance of
the spirit; blue is the radiance, the lustre of the soul, and red is the lustre of life.
These colours (although slightly modified by the bluish tone of the background)

1. *The Colour Lectures*, Lecture 4 - 'The Creative World of Colour', Dornach, 26 July, 1914.
2. Ibid. lectures 1, 2 and 3, given 6, 7, 8 May, 1921.

create an impression of the invisible etheric life-forces active within the plant.

The colouring of flowers in their beautiful variations, contrasts with the consistency of the predominantly green hues of all the leaves. What is taking place here? The flowering, and in fruits the ripening process, occur due to the influence of the sun's warmth and light. The sun transforms, or metamorphoses the green into various colours, which are in turn influenced by different planets affecting the variety of colours. We can see a wonderful interplay of sun and planets influencing flowers and fruit, whilst the moon influences the green leaves. The sun shines, radiating brightness and light. The lustrous colours of flowers also seem to shine when we compare them to the green leaves. Here we have an earthly reflection of what is taking place in the cosmos: sunlight shines, moonlight is an image reflecting the sun. Here we are able to enter into some of the visible, yet concealed secrets of the living world of nature and of plants, through this distinction of image and lustre colours.

In the painting we can also observe a violet-magenta colour, which is similar to peach-blossom, and we can discover a wonderful relationship to this colour through following a simple experiment.

1. Gaze on this green surface for about 30-40 seconds. It doesn't matter if you blink, but do keep your eyes constantly on the green colour.

2. Shift your gaze to the white surface, and focus for a few seconds.

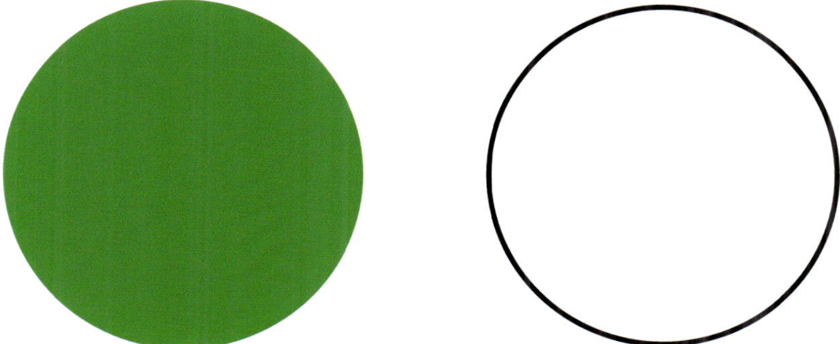

3. A luminous pale rose-pink colour should appear. If not, try again!

This luminous colour is an after-image. Our eyes create this colour as an inner balancing process in response to the outer sense impression. All colours produce after-images but it is this green-peach-blossom phenomena which we are interested in. Various shades of green will produce slightly different shades of peach-blossom, ranging from a glowing rosy-pink to a violet-magenta. This range of colours is also known as "'incarnate" or incarnadine, the image colour which Rudolf Steiner calls "the living image of the soul". This colour changes with the relationship of life and death processes within the human body. When the soul leaves the physical body, the rosy colour of the skin changes into its opposite, a greenish or yellowish hue. We can understand this colour to be intimately related to life, and is visible throughout the *Archetypal Plant* painting. Although the plant has no soul as such, we can experience the plant kingdom as being imbued and permeated with life-forces.

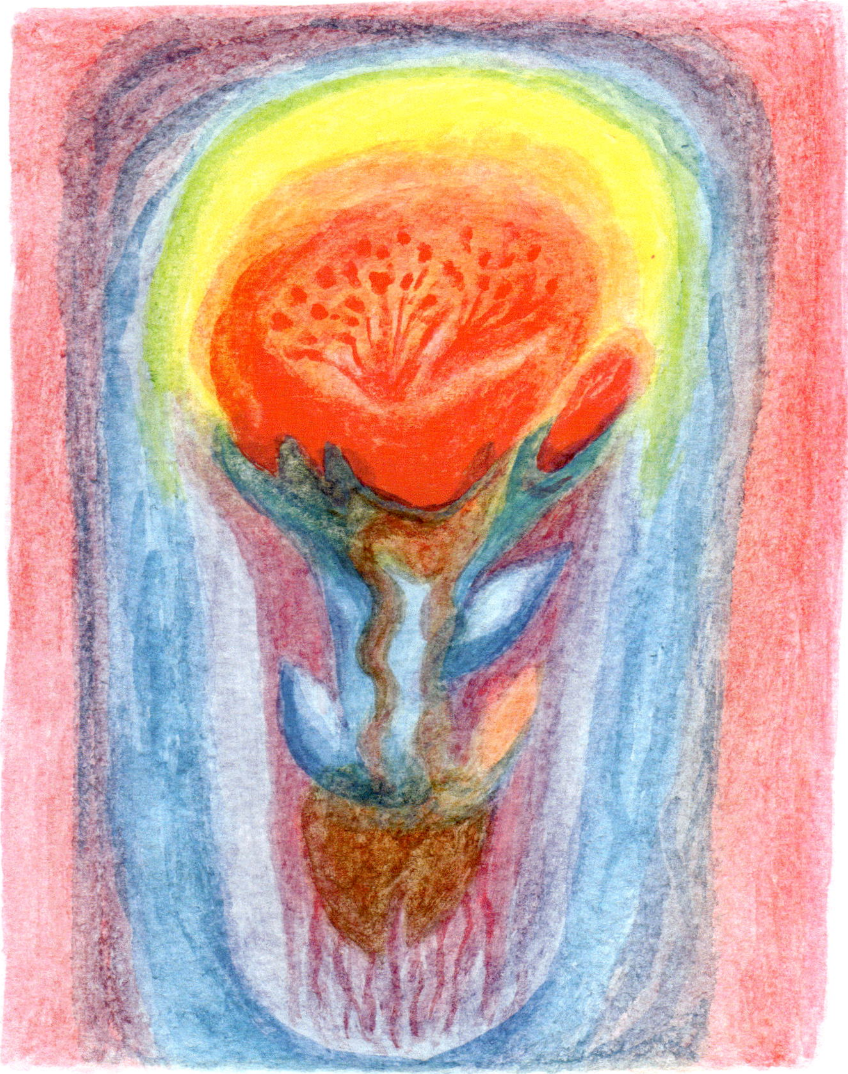

Fig. 31. *Archetypal Plant* (author)

CHAPTER THREE: AN APPROACH TO PAINTING THE MOTIF

"Thus it is a matter of discovering in painting the secret of creating after nature, out of the colours. For a great part of the reality we survey is in fact actually born out of the creative world of colour. As vegetation sprouted out of the sea, so everything living grows out of the colour world"

Rudolf Steiner, *Colour Lectures*

This book concludes with several examples of colour research processes. They are intended to give guidelines and to provide a methodological approach, which is needed when one attempts to "enter into" and understand Rudolf Steiner's motif artistically.

These few examples are included to encourage an adventurous, open-minded curiosity: how can I paint this image? What happens when I paint the image in different ways? What do I discover when I experiment with varying sequences of colour? Can I develop my own archetypal plant? How do these normally closed secrets of nature reveal themselves to me?

Example One:

1. Lemon yellow is brought onto the page. We can ask: How much yellow do I need so that it does not fill the whole page nor seem too small? What shape or form seems to express the sunny bright quality of yellow? Where on the page does yellow feel best? We can see that yellow has come into the upper picture space, where it seems to hover, expressing its light, luminous quality.

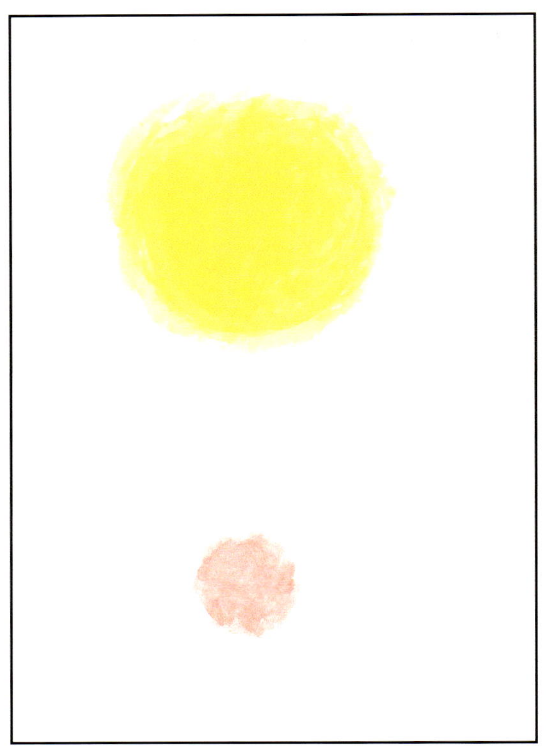

2. Brown is brought onto the paper. We can ask: How much brown do I need compared to the yellow? Does brown seem heavier, more dense? We can see that brown compared to yellow is a colour which has weight in it and is contracted. It comes naturally to the lower picture space and has a smaller denser surface.

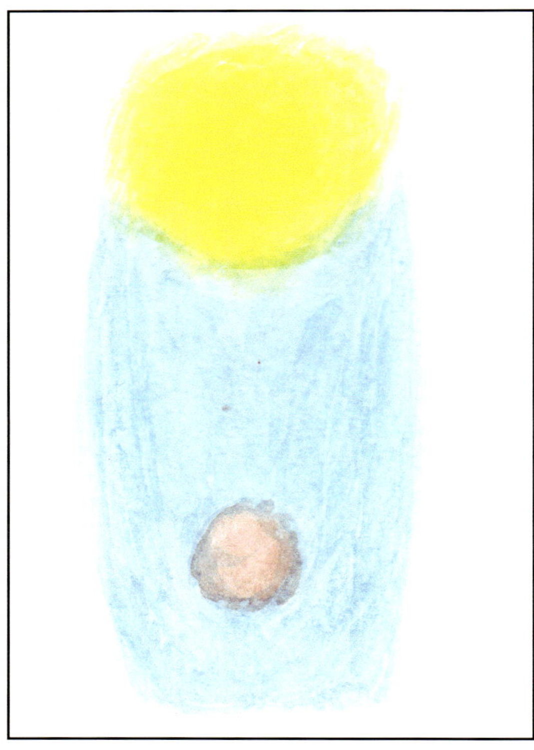

3. A pale cool blue surrounds the yellow and brown. The blue holds onto the yellow; the brown seems lighter, as the surrounding blue takes the light away from its surrounding. The blue weighs the yellow down and lightens the brown simultaneously. Is this the way water affects air? (yellow) Is this the way a seed begins to open and germinate? (brown)

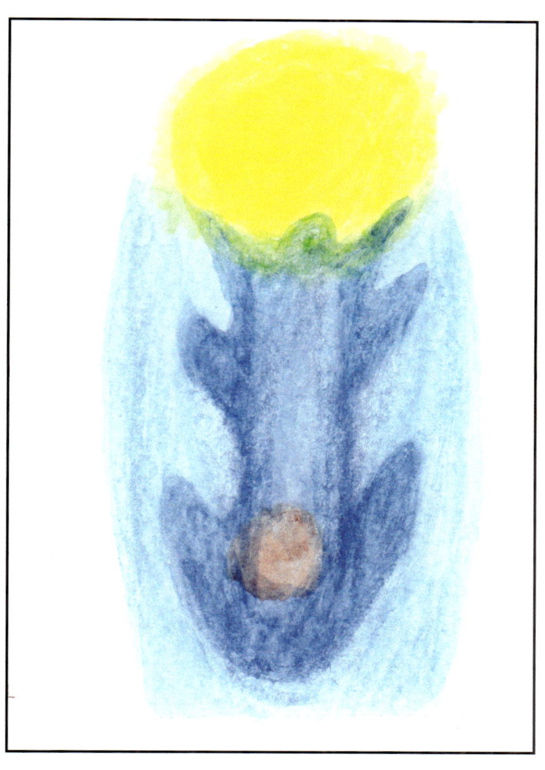

4. Indigo, or a strong prussian-blue, creates a dynamic movement between the brown and yellow. It has the strength to create forms. A budding process begins within the pale-blue water surrounding.

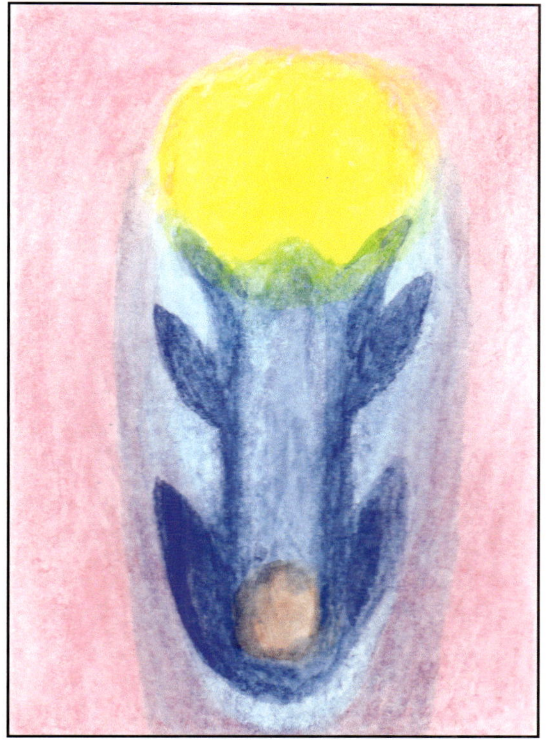

5. The one-sidedness of the cool atmosphere created by the two blues is balanced by a crimson-red or rose madder coming to the periphery. The plant feels protected in this colour.

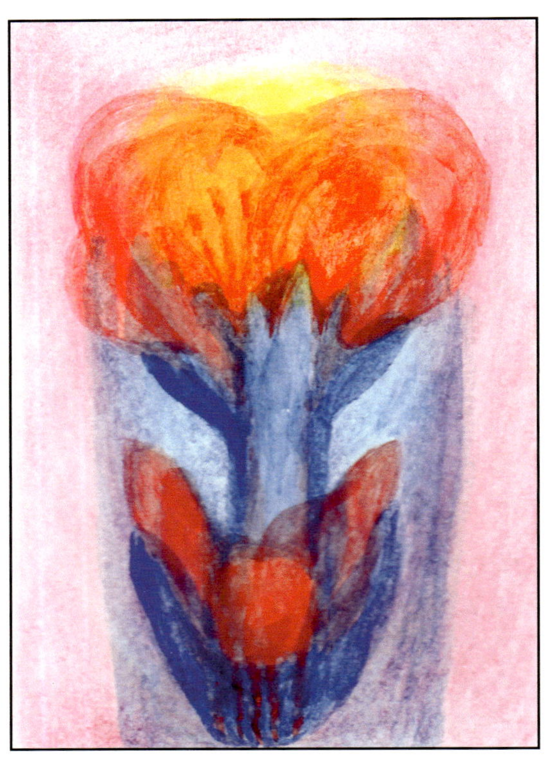

6. Warmth springs to life within the plant. We bring a warm red (scarlet or vermillion) which forms the flower, the buds, and comes into the bulb, as well as creating the roots.

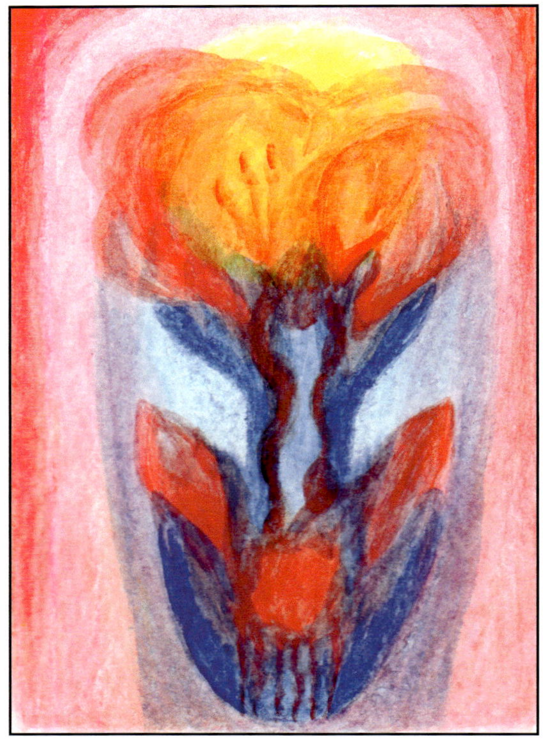

7. The warm red extends to the periphery and builds the inner structures within the stem. When red enters yellow, it remains luminous. When red enters the indigo stem, it darkens and densifies. We can ask: Is the red participating in several processes? The flowering is a result of cosmic influences; the inner structures are related to the carbon scaffolding, the carbon-structure processes within the stem.

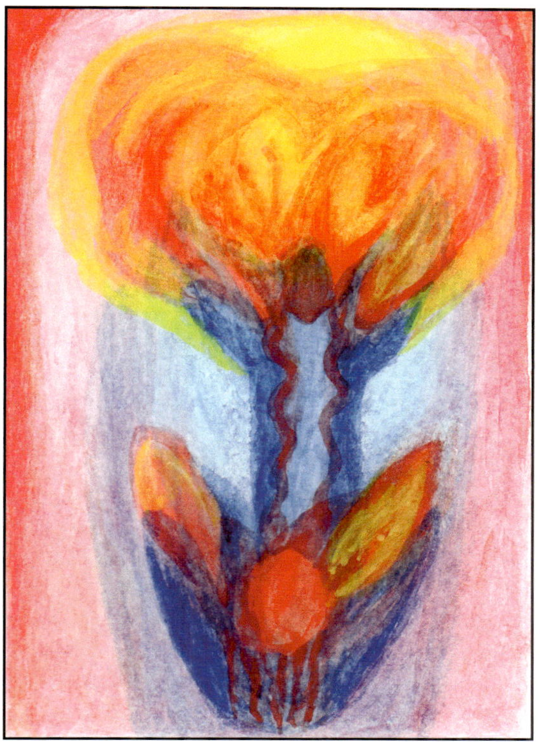

8. Yellow surrounds the flower, entering into the flower and into the buds. Here we can ask: Is a sulphur process at work, opening the flower and eventually allowing the flower to release itself into the cosmos?

<u>Colour Sequence</u> (6 colours are needed)

1. Lemon-yellow (cadmium-lemon)

2. Medium brown (burnt sienna, burnt umber, raw sienna, raw umber)

3. Pale cool blue (phthalo, pale prussian, cyan, cerulean)

4. Indigo (or prussian plus a little black)

5. Cool red (crimson, rose madder, carmine, magenta, alizarin)

6. Warm red (vermillion, scarlet, cadmium)

7. Medium yellow (winsor, cadmium-lemon, aureolin)

Seven colours are needed in total. The order of the colours (the colour sequence) is important as this determines the processes, the colour responses and interactions, and the motif itself.

Example Two

1. Lemon-yellow.

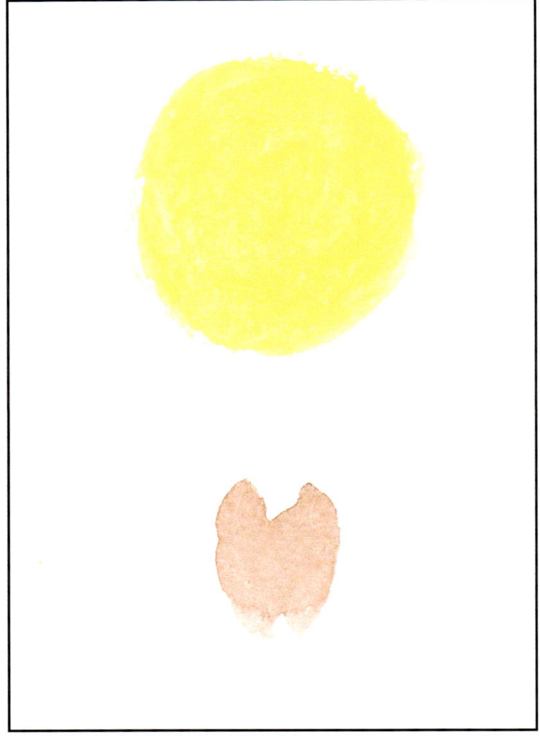

2. Brown. In this example, the brown is larger owing to its having more red in it. This makes it more active and expansive.

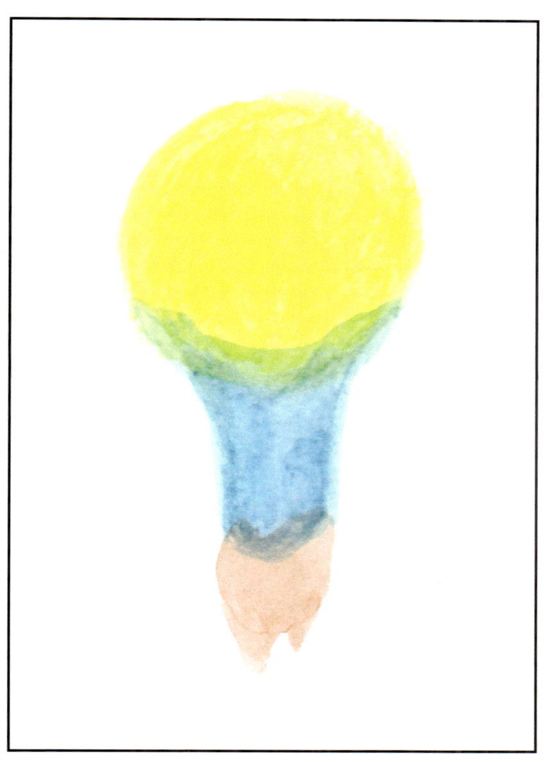

3. Indigo-blue (or strong prussian) creates a connecting stem, a simple structure between the upper yellow and the lower brown.

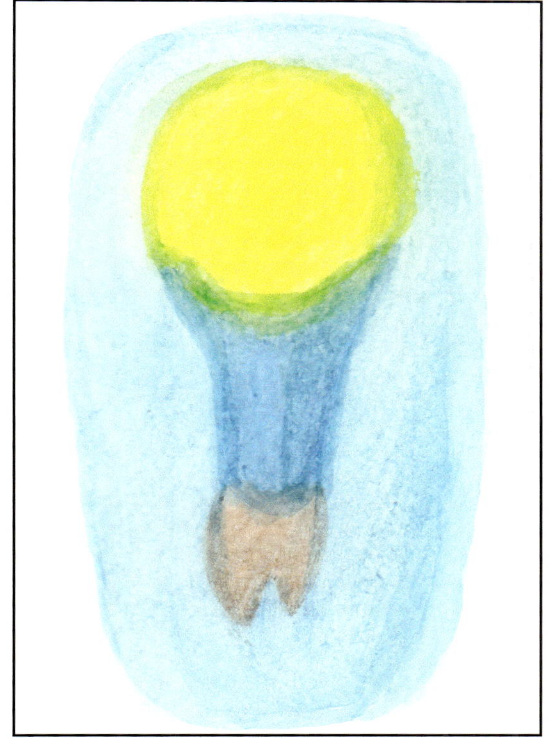

4. A paler blue surrounds the whole plant. (Pale prussian, cerulean, or phthalo blue.)

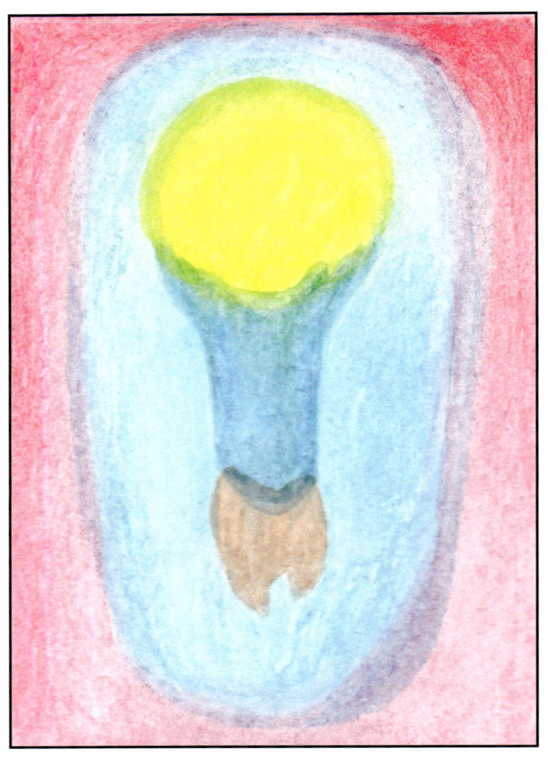

5. Cool red surrounds the blue. The whole image gains light (even the brown "opens up"). The colours become more transparent and open. I have used rose madder.

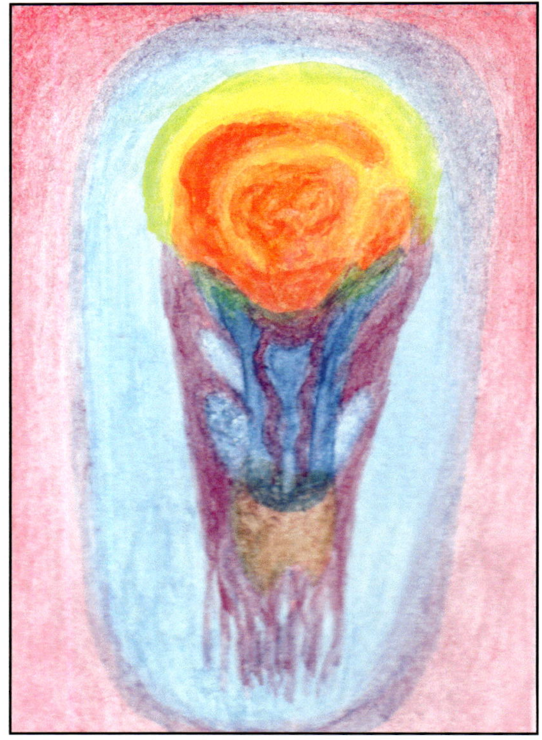

6. Cool red enters into all aspects of the plant – the stem, the flowers, the roots.

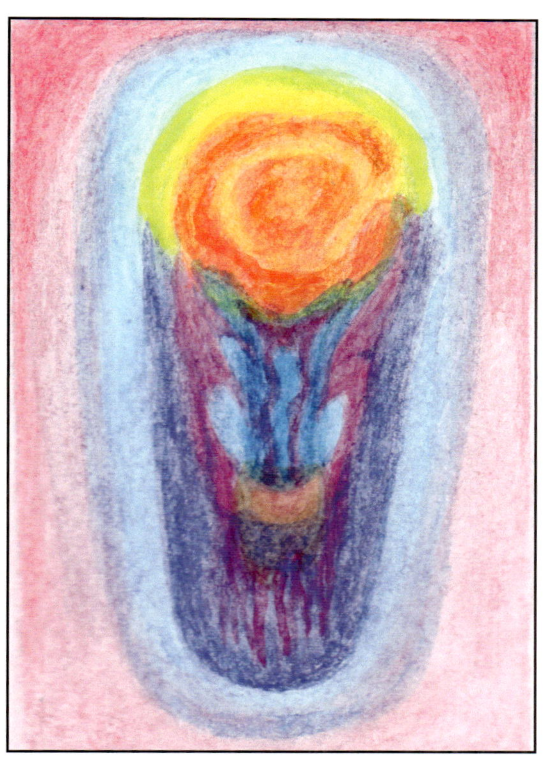

7. Ultramarine creates the watery sac surrounding the stem and roots.

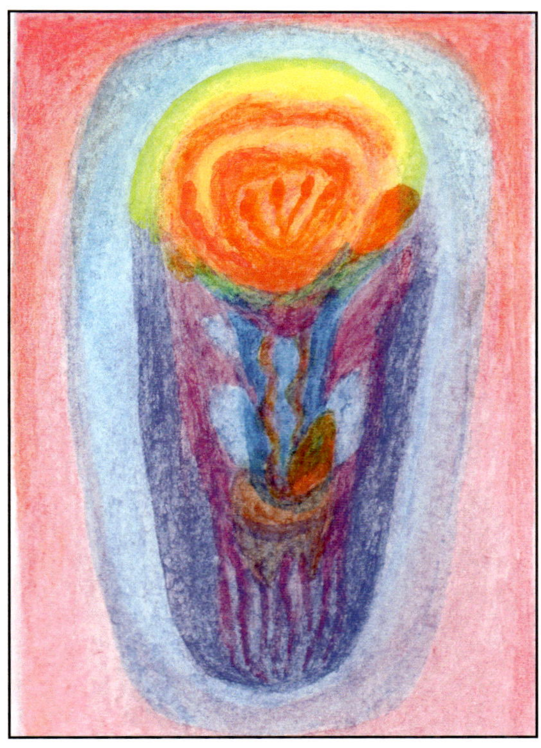

8. Warm red (vermillion or scarlet) – orange and lemon-yellow bring warmth and details to the plant.

<u>Colour sequence (8 colours)</u>

1. Lemon-yellow
2. Reddish brown
3. Indigo
4. Pale blue
5. Rose madder
6. Ultramarine
7. Vermillion
8. Orange
9. Lemon-yellow

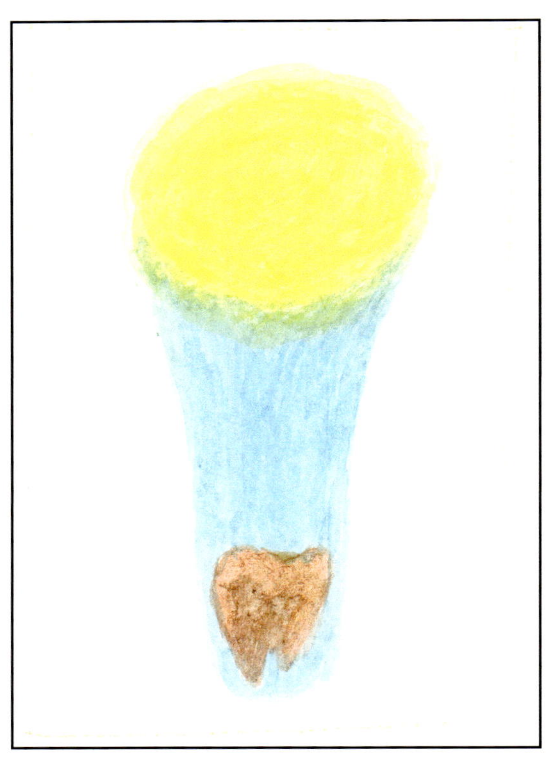

Example Three:

1. Yellow, brown and indigo (in the same sequence as example Two).

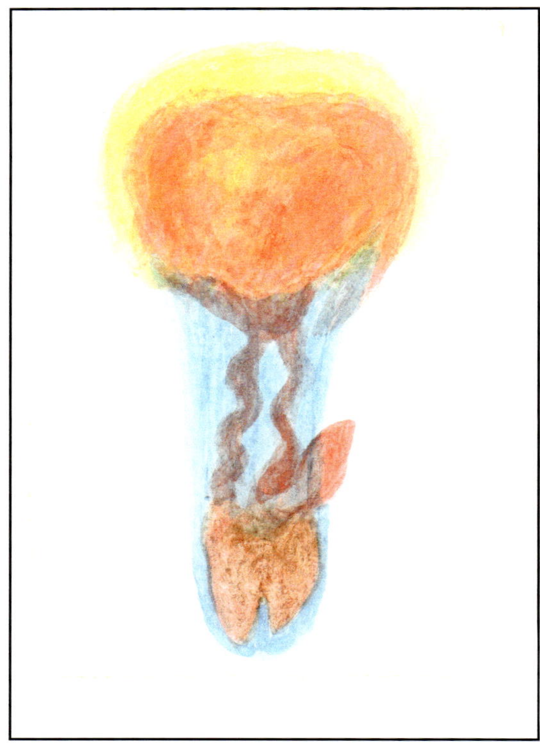

2. Warm red enters directly into the plant.

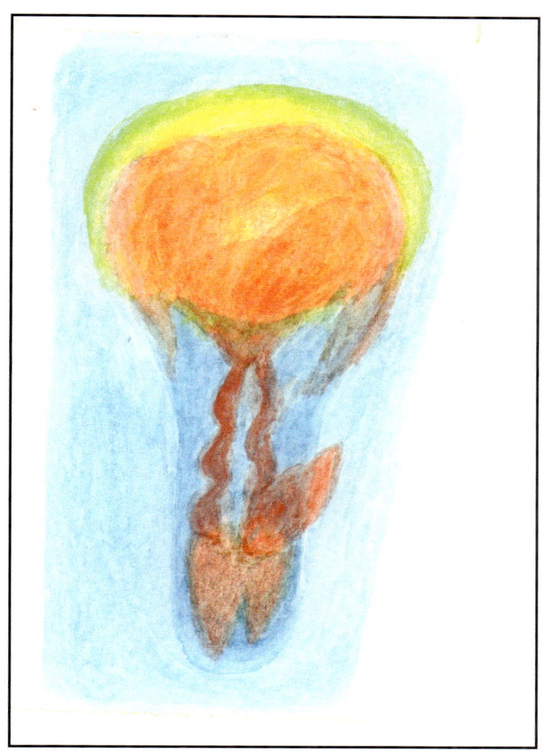

3. Cool blue surrounds the whole plant.

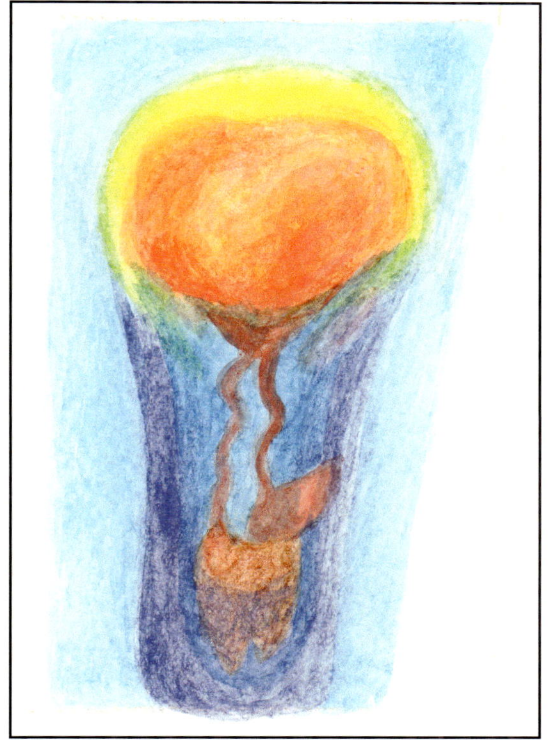

4. Ultramarine creates the watery sac.

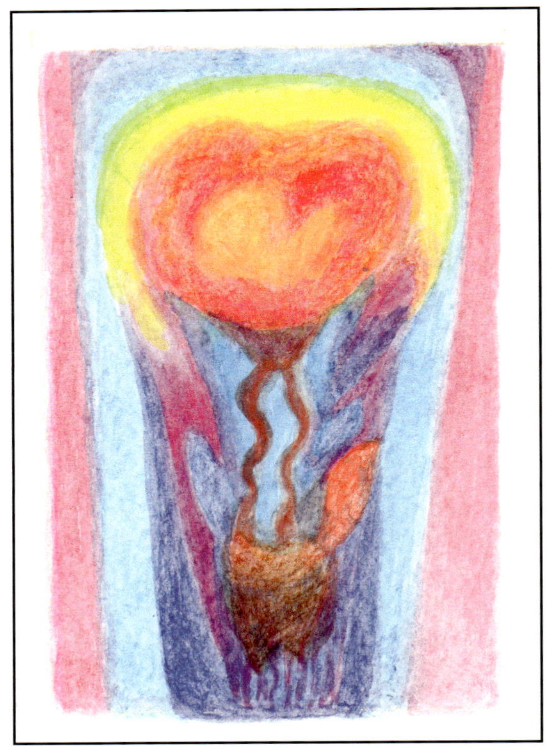

5. Rose madder comes to the outer periphery, opening the plant. It then enters into the ultramarine, forms the roots and enhances the flower and buds.

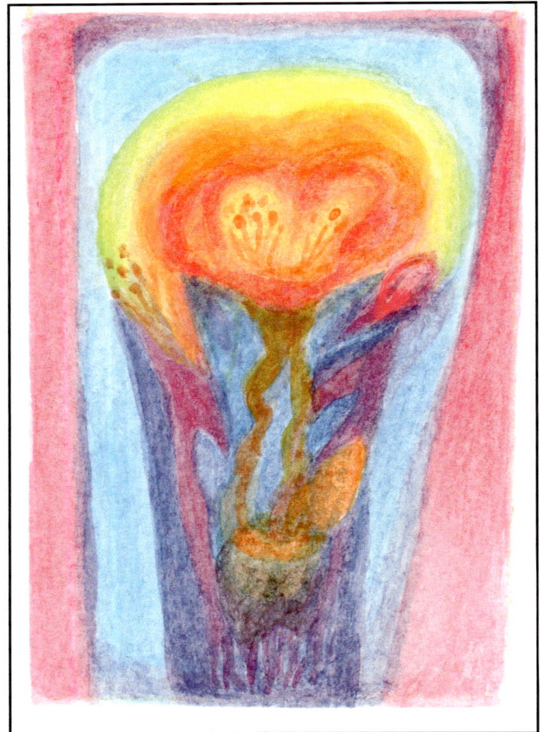

6. Orange creates details in the flowers.

<u>Colour sequence</u>

1. Lemon-yellow
2. Medium brown
3. Indigo (or prussian blue)
4. Vermillion
5. Pale blue
6. Ultramarine
7. Rose madder
8. Orange

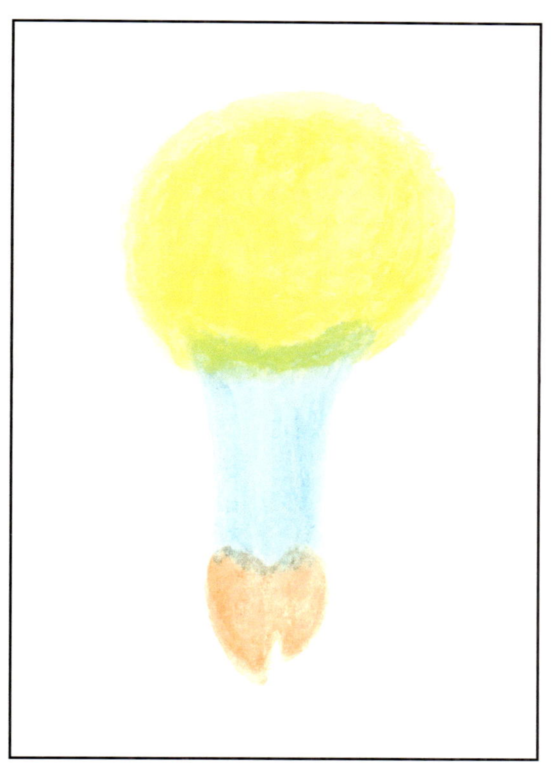

Example Four

1. Lemon-yellow – warm brown – indigo (or strong prussian blue).

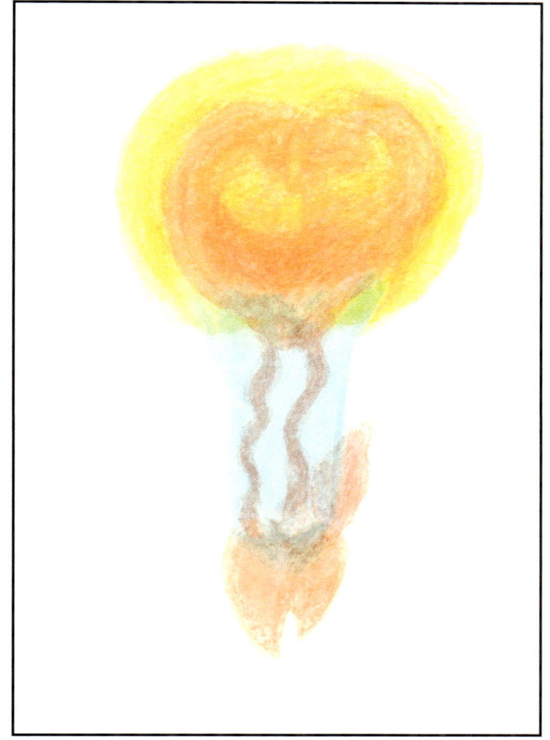

2. Warm red (vermillion or scarlet) creates the flower, buds, inner structures in the stem.

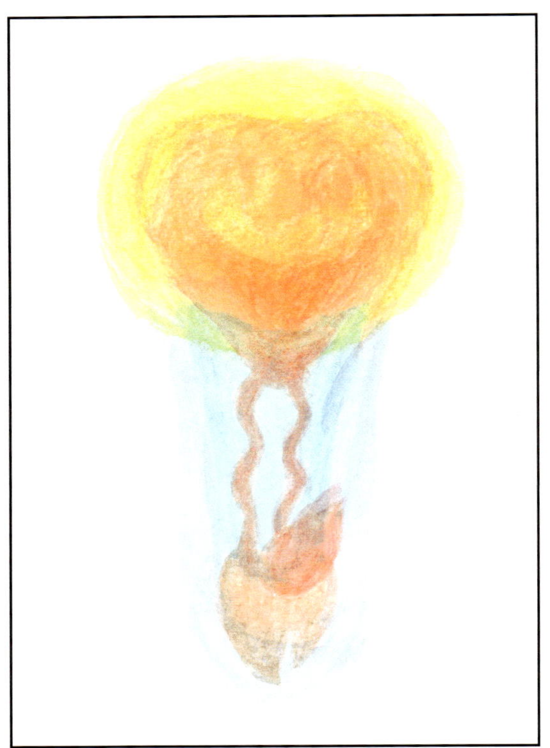

3. Ultramarine creates the watery sac.

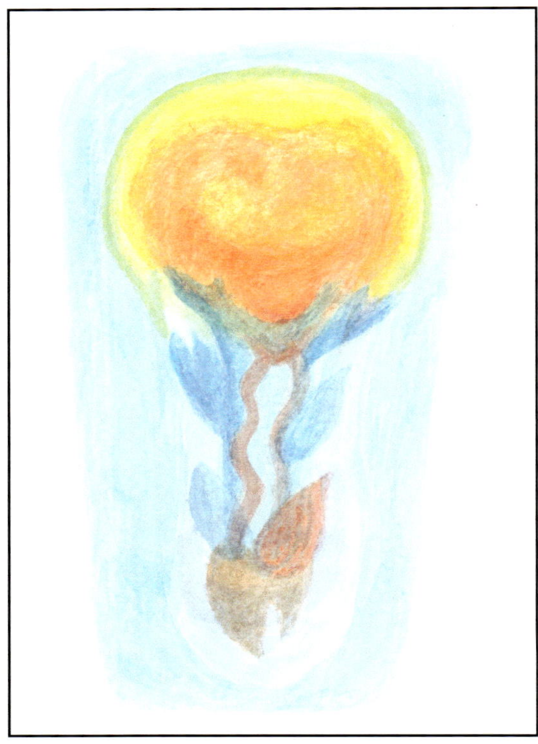

4. Cool blue (prussian, cerulean, phthalo blue) surrounds the whole plant and creates buds along the stem.

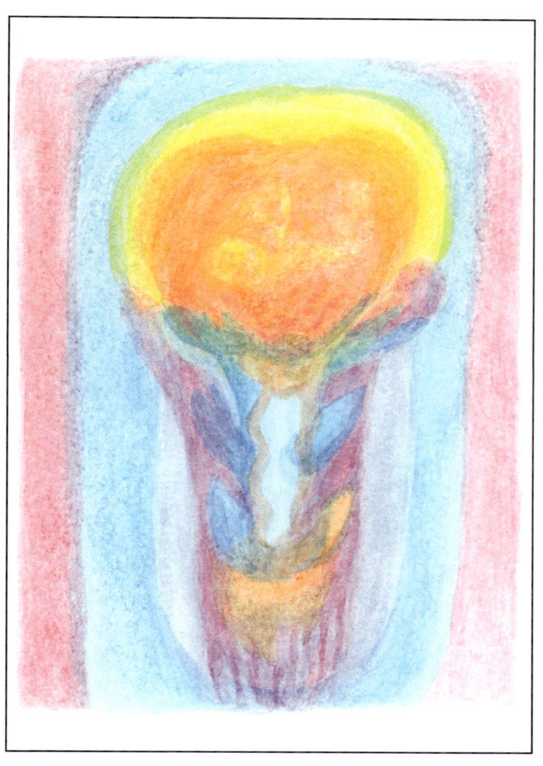

5. Rose madder (or crimson) enters the flower, the watery sac surrounding the stem, and forms the roots.

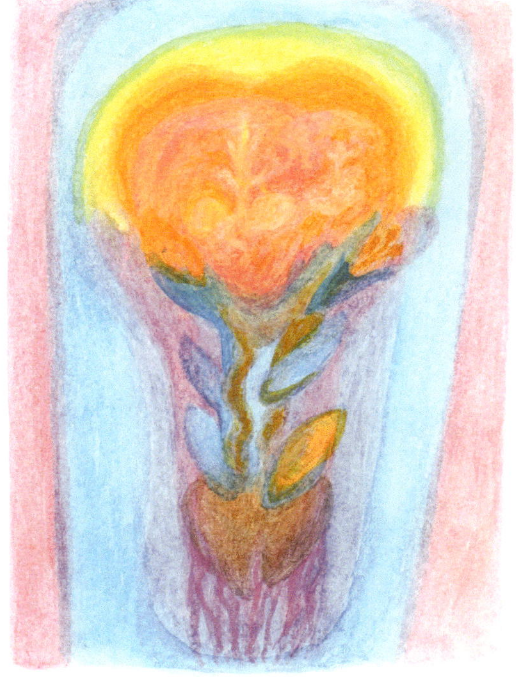

6. Orange brings liveliness and warmth to the buds and flower.

<u>Colour Sequence</u>

1. Lemon-yellow
2. Warm brown
3. Indigo (or prussian blue)
4. Vermillion
5. Ultramarine
6. Prussian blue
7. Rose madder
8. Orange

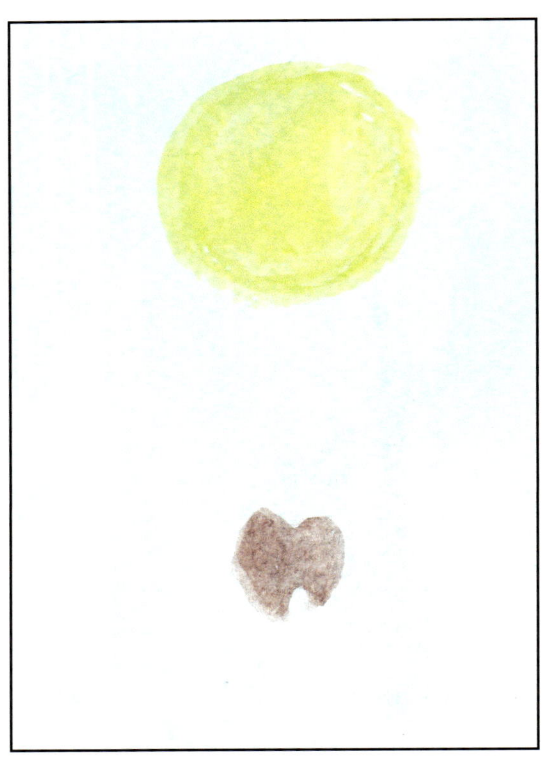

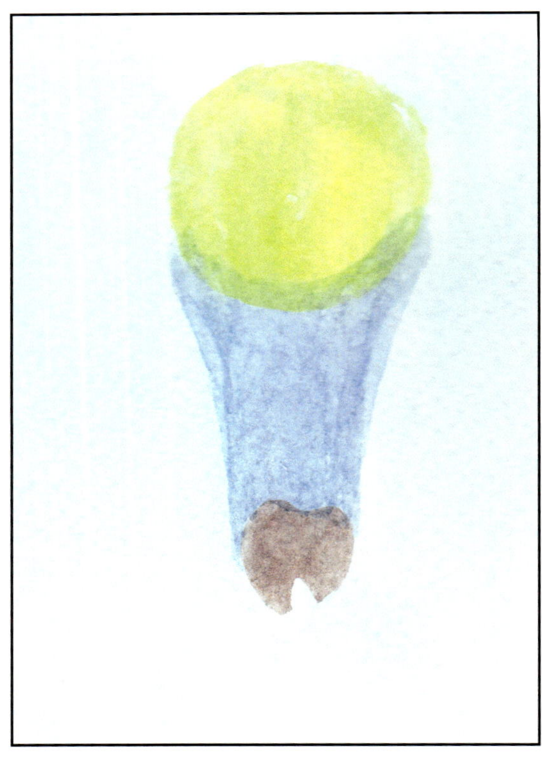

Example Five:

1. Tone the paper with a pale-blue wash, as evenly as possible, and allow to dry. (Pale prussian, cerulean, or phthalo blue.)

2. Lemon-yellow, brown and indigo come onto the blue-toned paper. They appear subdued in the blue atmosphere.

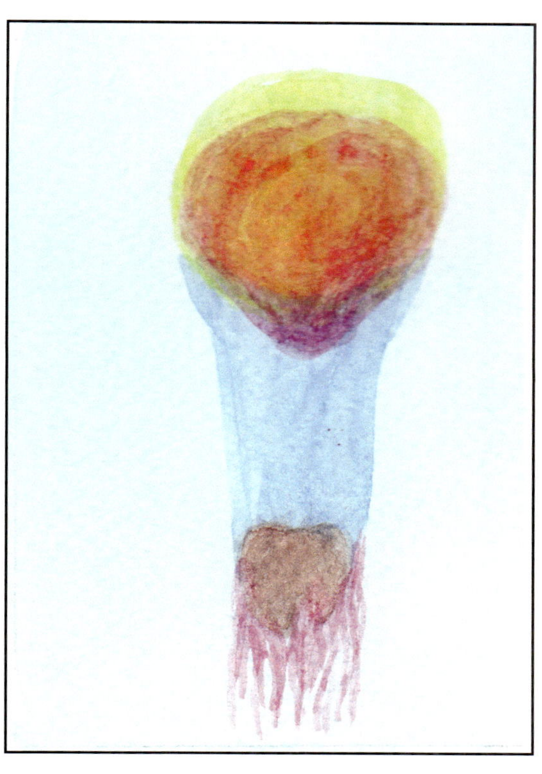

3. Rose madder (or crimson) creates the flower and roots. Here, one experiences a strong polarity of above and below. The central stem seems open and transparent.

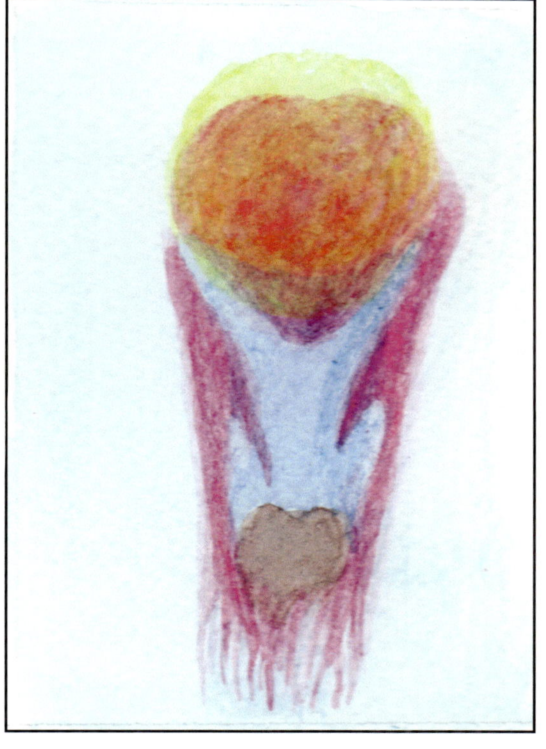

4. Rose madder (or crimson) surrounds the indigo, entering into the stem to create a dynamic movement between the red and the blue. The brown seems lighter.

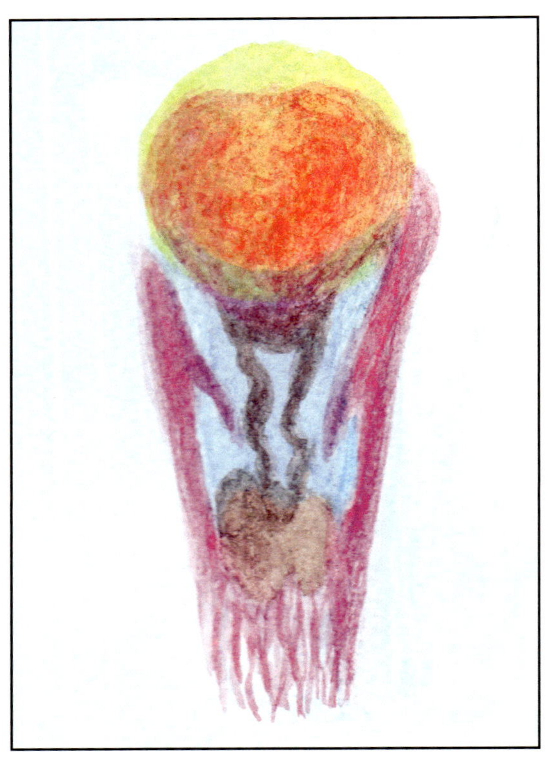

5. Brown can become active – it rises and forms the structures within the stem.

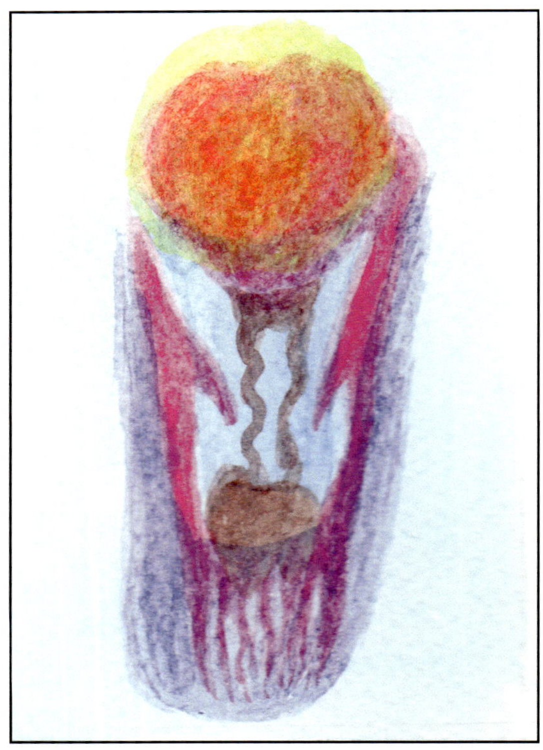

6. A violet-blue (mix blue and rose madder together) creates the watery sac.

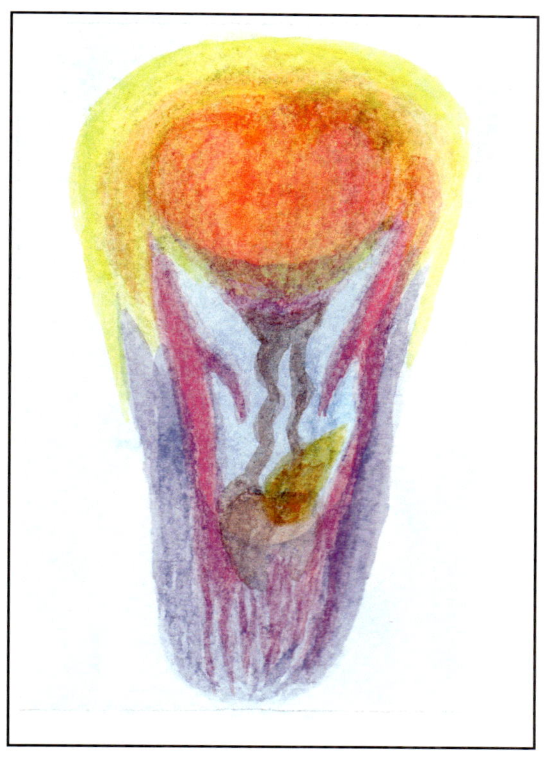

7. Warm yellow brings warmth to the cool red flower, and forms a bud near the bulb.

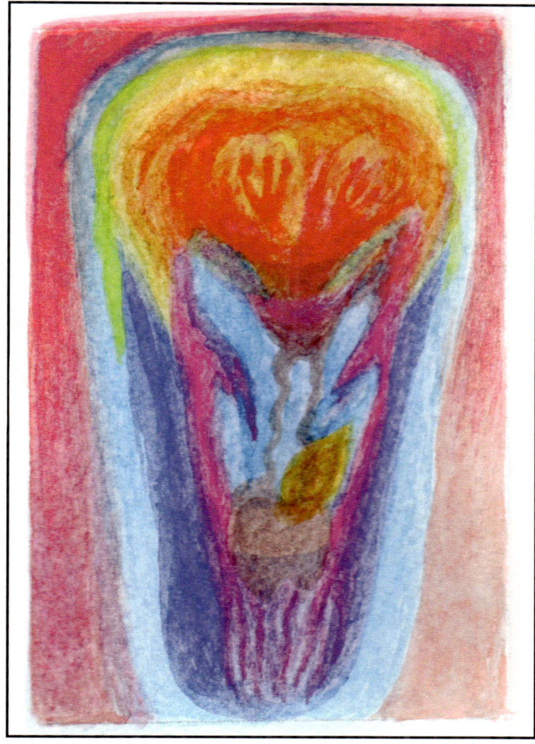

8. Vermillion comes to the periphery and into the centre of the flower. The pale blue has also been intensified.

<u>Colour Sequence (7 colours)</u>

1. Blue-toned paper
2. Lemon-yellow
3. Brown
4. Indigo
5. Rose madder
6. Brown
7. Violet blue
8. Warm yellow (golden yellow)
9. Vermillion
10. Prussian blue (cerulean/phthalo)

REFERENCES AND BIBLIOGRAPHY

An Introduction to Celtic Mythology, David Bellingham. Publ. Sandstone Books, Australia, 1990.

Ancient Mexican Art, Ferdinand Anton. Publ. Thames and Hudson, London.

Christian Symbols, Heather Child and Dorothy Colles. Publ. Bell and Hyman, London, 1971.

Larousse Dictionary of World Folklore, Alison Jones. Publ. Larousse plc, 1995.

Living with Invisible People, Jostein Saether. Publ. Clairview Books, 2001.

New Larousse Encyclopedia of Mythology, publ. Paul Hamlyn, England, 1970.

New View Magazine, Summer 2006.

The Vortex of Life, Lawrence Edwards. Publ. Floris Books, 1993.

The Golden Blade Journal, 1988.

The Individuality of Colour, Elizabeth Koch/Gerard Wagner. Publ. Rudolf Steiner Press, 1980.

The Dictionary of the Esoteric, Nevill Drury. Publ. Watkins, London.

The Plant Between Sun and Earth, Olive Whicher/George Adams. Publ. Rudolf Steiner Press, London, 1980.

The Green Man, Kathleen Basford. Publ. D. S. Brewer Ltd 1978.

The Bible, King James' Revised Standard Version.

Centres of Belief (The Grand Tour), Flavio Conti. Publ. Cassell, London 1977.

The Lost Meaning of Classical Architecture, George Hersey. Publ. The MIT Press, Cambridge, Massachusetts, USA.

Three Books of Occult Philosophy – The Foundation of Western Occultism, Henry Cornelius Agrippa. Transl. by James Freake, edited by Donald Tyson. Publ. Llewellyn's Sourcebook Series, USA, 2003.

Gerard Wagner – Catalogue of the Exhibition in November 1997 at the State Hermitage, St Petersburg. Publ. Novikoff Press, 1997.

Gerard Wagner - *Farbenwesen und Urpflanze Metamorphosen* reproduced from *Die Drei* Journal No. 7-8, 1990.

<u>Rudolf Steiner</u>

The Calendar of the Soul, transl. Hans and Ruth Pusch.

Agriculture Lectures, publ. Biodynamic Agriculture Assoc. biodynamic.org.uk.

Verses and Meditations, publ. Rudolf Steiner Press.

Goethe's World View, publ. Mercury Press.

Man as Symphony of the Creative Word, Rudolf Steiner Press.

The Influence of Spiritual Beings Upon Man, Anthroposophic Press, Spring Valley, New York.

The Festivals and their Meanings, Rudolf Steiner Press.

Cosmic Memory: Atlantis and Lemuria, publ. SteinerBooks, 1959, New York, USA.

Wonders of the World, publ. Rudolf Steiner Press, London, 1963. Ten lectures given in Munich, 18-27 Aug., 1911.

Colour, publ. Rudolf Steiner Press, Sussex, 1992.